PRAISE FOR *LEMONS ON FRIDAY*

"When a tea bag gets steeped in hot water, the true content and nature of what's inside the bag, whether sweet or bitter, is revealed. The same is true of people when their lives become steeped in unexpected sorrow and loss. I will never forget how the sweet aroma of Christ, even and especially through honest yet noncynical, humble tears, came out of Mattie when she lost her beloved husband, Ben. I am thankful that she has gone more public with her story, so that others can see in it the goodness of God in times when they need him most."

—SCOTT SAULS, SENIOR PASTOR OF CHRIST PRESBYTERIAN CHURCH
AND AUTHOR OF *JESUS OUTSIDE THE LINES* AND *A GENTLE ANSWER*

"Mattie's story carries you through a valley of unbearable heartbreak, and in the very next moment you are experiencing an ocean of peace that is the heartbeat of Jesus. Her honesty and vulnerability in this book are a beacon of light to any heart that has experienced total darkness. The courage and wisdom expressed through her words will inspire hope in readers, no matter their walk of life."

—LAUREN AKINS, AUTHOR OF THE *NEW YORK TIMES* BESTSELLER
LIVE IN LOVE: GROWING TOGETHER THROUGH LIFE'S CHANGES

"There is a sisterhood among all of us who have been widowed at far too young of an age. That's where our story intersected with Mattie's. She's wonderful, witty, and wise beyond her years. In *Lemons on Friday* she takes us all on a journey that is less about making lemonade out of lemons and more about looking to faith for transformational healing. Her story of loss, with hope, reminds us that partnering with Christ can turn the bitter sorrows of life into something far sweeter than we could ever accomplish on our own."

—RACHEL BROWN AND GINGER RAVELLA, FOUNDERS,
BE STILL MINISTRIES AND NEVER ALONE WIDOWS RETREATS

"An honest and vulnerable peek into the healing spaces between love, grief, hope, growth, and true restoration. Attainable by all, through God's mercy and grace, especially for the 258 million widows globally we are called to care for in their distress. This is an answer to that divine call."

—CAROLYN MOOR, FOUNDER, MODERN WIDOWS CLUB

"The most honest, vulnerable, and completely beautiful look inside loss and grief. Mattie's courage to share her intimate thoughts on love, death, grief, and her unending faith will be a gift to those who have loved and those who grieve. Only someone who has suffered through the death of a loved one can write from this place. *Lemons on Friday* is a lifeline for those who have suffered loss and those who seek to find joy in life again."

—LIZ ALLISON, NASCAR ANALYST, AUTHOR, AND RADIO HOST

"Too often, as Christians, we have no idea how to approach grief. We either stuff it down, dismiss it, 'Jesus juke' one another, or end up drowning in it. The church needs Mattie's story because, through it, she teaches us something about what it looks like to grieve honestly but with hope."

—RACHEL JOY WELCHER, EDITOR AT *FATHOM* MAGAZINE
AND AUTHOR OF *TALKING BACK TO PURITY CULTURE*

"*Lemons on Friday* is a beautiful and raw depiction of what grief can look like and a hopeful testament to how God can take life's most painful situations and weave them into an incredible masterpiece. Mattie is a wonderfully gifted writer and storyteller whose ability to capture the roller coaster of loss and faith in God's promises is unparalleled."

—SHANNON FRAZIER, MMFT (MARRIAGE AND FAMILY THERAPIST)

"No matter what the format—songs, books, and so on—writing allows us to share experiences with and enter into the lives of people we may never meet face to face. For all those who pick up this book, they are welcomed into Mattie's personal story of heartbreak and are reminded in the midst of their own pain: you are not alone, and hope is never really out of reach."

—LEE ANN WOMACK, GRAMMY-WINNING, ACM-WINNING, AND CMA-WINNING RECORDING ARTIST

LEMONS
ON
FRIDAY

LEMONS ON FRIDAY

TRUSTING GOD THROUGH MY GREATEST HEARTBREAK

MATTIE JACKSON SELECMAN

W PUBLISHING GROUP

AN IMPRINT OF THOMAS NELSON

Published in Nashville, Tennessee, by W Publishing, an imprint of Thomas Nelson.

Thomas Nelson titles may be purchased in bulk for educational, business, fundraising, or sales promotional use. For information, please email SpecialMarkets@ThomasNelson.com.

ISBN 978-0-7852-4133-1 (audiobook)
ISBN 978-0-7852-4132-4 (eBook)
ISBN 978-0-7852-4127-0 (HC)

Library of Congress Cataloging-in-Publication Data

Library of Congress Control Number: 2021938879

Printed in the United States of America
21 22 23 24 25   LSC   10 9 8 7 6 5 4 3 2 1

For Ben, my "Adam," faithful though flawed and abounding in selfless love. You loved with your whole heart and without expectation. Through both your life and death, the Lord has worked immeasurable good in me. Forever, your "Eve."

CONTENTS

FOREWORD

Even when Mattie was a toddler, Alan and I marveled at her use of language and her ability to articulate. So did others she came in contact with, from the shoe store clerk who literally gasped and said, "That baby can *talk*!" when our eighteen-month-old baby tried on a pair of shoes and exclaimed, "Too tight!" to the loud ovation Mattie received after her inspiring high school graduation valedictory address to her peers. Throughout her youth, family members as well as friends and acquaintances have often said of Mattie, "She is wise beyond her years."

Mattie has always loved language and learning, so it was no surprise to us that she chose English with a focus on creative writing as her college major. After finishing college, Mattie shared with us that she wanted to be a book writer—again, no surprise. Alan very wisely gave her this advice: "Mattie, you are a talented writer, but you need to go live life first. Then you'll have something to write about." And that's exactly what she did.

After college, she moved to Austin, Texas, started working in the food and wine industry, enjoyed a season in Napa working for a prestigious winery, and ultimately studied to get her certification as a sommelier (a certified wine specialist). After a few years away, she moved back to Nashville with a vision and a dream of opening her own restaurant and bottle shop. She successfully built Salt & Vine from the ground up and served as its owner from June 2016 to June 2018.

During those hectic years as a restaurant owner, Mattie met Ben—and long story short, they married within two years of their first date. Ben was everything we as parents had prayed for for Mattie: a man of integrity who loved the Lord; a smart, young lawyer with a budding career; a handsome outdoorsman who lived life to the fullest, loved others wholeheartedly, and, above all, loved and adored Mattie with all of his heart and soul. Their marriage was a beautiful love story and tangible evidence of our answered prayers.

All was well with our newlyweds until three weeks before their first anniversary, when a tragic accident took Ben's life. The depth of shock, pain, and grief that followed for our family and Ben's was almost unbearable.

This book was birthed out of Mattie's devastating heartbreak of losing her adoring twenty-eight-year-old husband and, with that loss, all of their plans and dreams to live happily ever after together. Mattie vulnerably and intimately shares her personal journey of grief and loss—their love story, the accident, the twelve days by his hospital bedside, the confusion of unanswered prayers, and, ultimately, the healing and renewed hope she found in Jesus.

The night before Ben's passing, after we had gotten the devastating doctor's report that Ben had suffered massive strokes and would not recover, I screamed and cried out to God in anger and desperation, "Why have you not answered our fervent prayers for Ben's earthly healing when you could have? His death will *not* be in vain! This had better be so big for your kingdom, Lord!" What you hold in your hands is just one confirmation to us as parents that my prayer is beginning to be answered and proof that God often uses great heartbreak and loss to reveal his unfolding purposes and will for our lives.

No parents would ever wish this kind of grief and heartbreak on their child. We would turn back time in a second if we could. But we can already see how our loving heavenly Father is using Mattie's story for good and for his purposes—and we know that Ben's legacy of faith will live on through her words. Our hope is that as you read this book, you too will find healing, comfort, and the renewed hope that Mattie has found—and ultimately, the God of hope himself.

—Denise and Alan Jackson

INTRODUCTION

Aren't all these notes the senseless writhings
of a man who won't accept the fact that there is
nothing we can do with suffering except to suffer
it? Who still thinks there is some device (if only he
could find it) which will make pain not to be pain.

C. S. LEWIS, *A GRIEF OBSERVED*

G rief doesn't come with a handbook. If you've lost someone dear to you, this idea has either offered you freedom from the false expectation that there is a right way to grieve or it has left you feeling hopeless and without direction, reminding you day after day that you can't fix it, you can't define it, and you sure as hell can't defer it.

There are guidelines, of course—clinical scales that help determine phases of denial, anger, acceptance, and a few others. And while a useful tool, serving in some ways as an emotional mile marker, these scales follow anything but a linear order. Grief invokes chaos, shuffling these "steps" and "phases" out of line and often leaving us disoriented and internally off-balance. Grief is not a one-way street toward healing. We can't climb a ladder or check off boxes to reach a better day. Everyone's grief, and every day of grief, looks different. My pain is processed differently than yours, and our stories won't play out the same way. But what is true for most who have experienced grief is that the illusion of control over our lives—the tight, self-preserving grip we thought we held on our person and on our plans—is now gone. What we thought was secure has been snatched away.

For some, that may offer relief. After months or years marked by sickness, you're no longer the caretaker for an illness or an injury you couldn't control to begin with. Your loved one is no longer in pain, and you're released. For others, this wake-up call to unforeseen suffering breaks our hearts and confirms in life-changing ways that we are no longer, and never have been, in charge of our own fates.

The point is this: we all have different stories, struggles, fears, and feelings. We all stand at different points in faith, if even in faith at all. Some of us are years of tears past the days that wrecked and reset our lives. For some of us the loss is so fresh, we can't remember what it's like not to feel raw.

Today, at age thirty-one, I stand somewhere in between. Three weeks before our first wedding anniversary, I lost my husband to a sudden traumatic brain injury. Until then, my life had run pretty smoothly. I had a secure, loving family. Lifelong friends who'd grown to be more like sisters. A fairly successful career and a new marriage to a man who loved bigger and harder than I ever dreamed someone could. Up until that point, grief to me meant losing a grandparent or a friend moving to a new city. Both of which are absolutely painful, of course, but nothing had ever shattered my reality and my understanding of faith and suffering like losing Ben.

It's important you know my story is exactly that: a story. A true story of loss, heartbreak, and grieving a love and a life I'd planned for myself. A true story of a young woman who grew up in faith but who, in grappling with faith after loss, grew up in more ways than she could have imagined. I'm not going to give you clinical instruction on how to grieve. I'm not going to give you a polished picture of suffering with a pretty Christian bow on top. But I am going to tell you the truth about how I wrestled with a God who is absolutely good but who absolutely did not give me the miracle I prayed for. I'm going to share with you the ways I was courageous and the ways that I crumbled. I'm going to tell you a story of real lament, real confusion, and real hope. I'm going to tell you a story of the real God who has never left my side and who has transformed me through my suffering in more ways than ever before.

I don't know your pain or your story. But I do know that when we lose someone or something dear to us and we believe in a sovereign God, there are a few paths we can take. First, we can blame God and turn from faith. We can relinquish hope, weep alone, numb the pain, and resist moving forward in a desperate attempt to keep alive the presence of whomever or whatever we lost. But that, my friends, is the Enemy's dream—a paradise for the Evil One in which God's broken children sit abandoned by the Almighty who could have spared us this disaster. A self-enlisted army of the wounded, shaking fists at God for the miracle he didn't deliver. We play right into the Enemy's welcoming, conniving hands because God didn't play into ours. Nothing feels more vindicating than vowing, *I'll show you, God!* But refusing chemotherapy because you're angry you have cancer does as little to heal sickness as rejecting the Lord does to heal grief.

Second, we can be bullied by false expectations that faithful people need to "suck it up" because everything happens for a reason. In an attempt to be obedient, we deny the pain or mask how desperately broken we are. We think, *Maybe if I move forward quickly enough, I can outrun the worst of it. Maybe if I don't express how betrayed I feel by God, I can still trust him.* For many of us, the hardest thing to do is to lay down our pride and acknowledge our hurt—with God, with the circumstances, with our own helplessness.

These two paths are naturally human, but they will not lead us to healing. But there is a third way: we can be honest about how betrayed we feel by God because we don't understand—and also choose to trust God because we *can't* understand.

When life gives us lemons, only a long, grueling process can turn them into lemonade. It hurts every step of the way because the process is dependent on God's plan and God's timing, which almost always play out differently than we'd like. This book charts my day-to-day battle with a life turned suddenly sour and a faith that often left me feeling as abandoned as the disciples on crucifixion Friday. Jesus had left them even though he promised to be with them always. They felt alone and unsure and wanted to believe that all the promises Jesus had made them were true. They were grieving and lost.

Just as they did, we, too, will see he never really left, and his promises *are* true.

I didn't get the miracle I wanted. I prayed scriptures, sang hymns, and praised God in the ICU even after I was told my husband was brain-dead—and God still let Ben go. He didn't offer bodily healing to my Ben any more than he did for his Son left hanging on a cross. God wept that day too—over death and over his grieving daughter. He was wrecked by pain that a Father who lost a Son knows all too well.

Our God knows the deepest caverns of sorrow. He gets it. He hates it. But take heart from what I have experienced firsthand to be true: he still has everything we need to soothe and heal our tattered hearts. He loves us to depths that we simply cannot understand. Please allow him to heal you in all the ways you can't heal yourself.

I want to invite you into my journey through widowhood and grief because no matter what your valley looks like, you are not intended to brave it alone. Counseling, community, and times of disconnection from the world and connection with nature were crucial in treating both my emotional anguish and my cognitive trauma. But these things will look different and work differently for each of us. No matter what trial you're facing, it will be a fight. There's no getting around that. But if you are a follower of Christ, it's a fight he has already won. Praise Jesus! He delivered the world from universal sin; he can deliver us through this season of suffering.

The only "how-to" I've come up with in grief is how to rest in the Lord—rest in his provision and goodness and plan for the future. The future we thought was blissfully in place is no longer in our hands, but it was never really in our hands to begin with. It was always in God's hands—his loving, victorious, almighty hands. What better hands to take hold of the wheel, assume his rightful place in the driver's seat, and lead us through the chaos?

That's exactly where we're headed on our journey together—through the chaos, not around it. I'll pull back the curtain on my first years navigating the greatest devastation of my life. I'll shine light on where I fought, where I failed, and where I found the kind

Our God
knows the
deepest
caverns of
sorrow.

———

of peace that no human effort can explain. I'll invite you to walk with me as I've walked with the Lord through the darkness.

Much like the apostle Paul admitted to the Corinthians in his letter to their church, I am not coming to you "with lofty speech or wisdom" (1 Corinthians 2:1). I am coming to you "in weakness and in fear and with much trembling" (1 Corinthians 2:3 NET). If you are looking for an expert on grief, a PhD with profound theories and tricks to disarm loss and sorrow, stop reading now.

My nature is to study, fight, and create plans and strategies for success. I even walked into my first therapy session expecting a timeline. My counselor was kind not to refer me elsewhere right then. But after kicking the illusion that I could manage or defeat my grief, I surrendered. I accepted the chaos, put my name atop the list of those for whom I would have grace, and gave it to God. I literally threw up my hands and said, "You have it. Hold me, restore me, and make me the miracle." And one day at a time—some glorious and some agonizingly fragile—he has.

So I'm not here to offer sage how-tos or steps or solutions. I'm not here to motivate or pity or preach (okay, a little). I'm here to share with you my walk through the most harrowing valley of my life. I'm here to reach a tender hand into your story and your struggle and remind you that you're not in it alone. I'm here to assure you that while it feels impossible now, nothing is impossible with God, including healing and restoration and renewed life. I'm here to plead with you: grasp for the light; don't succumb to the darkness. And don't for one minute despair that the time for God to rescue you has run out.

Our stories may differ, but our Savior is the same. Dear sisters and brothers, let's lock arms, be kind to our broken selves, and tell the whole truth about our pain. Let's celebrate that joy and pain are not mutually exclusive. And let's surrender our hurts to the one Source who can truly heal.

I sincerely hope you find bits of peace and hope through my story, and I pray that the God of all healing makes a miracle out of yours.

one

FOR BETTER OR WORSE

HOW DID I GET HERE?

So they are no longer two but one
flesh. What therefore God has joined
together, let not man separate.
MATTHEW 19:6

When Ben and I got married, we chose to take traditional
wedding vows rather than write our own—partly because,
as he argued, my vows would be better than his. But mostly because we knew committing our lives to each other was more than
just formalizing the sentimental feelings of love; it was ultimately
the most life-changing choice we would ever make. We were prom-
ising the good, the bad, and the ugly parts of life to each other in

front of the people who had raised us, loved us, and helped shape us into two individuals choosing to become one.

The day was truly a dream. It was a mostly crisp October day (until a few brief rain showers came through), and I got to say "I do" to the love of my life right outside of my parents' home in Franklin, Tennessee. A stunning stone house perched atop one of Middle Tennessee's forested, rolling hills, it was the grandest yet most personal place we could have begun our life together.

We did a first look before the ceremony simply because we couldn't wait. I knew Ben would be far too emotional if the first time he saw me was coming down the aisle, and I also knew that I didn't want to wait until five o'clock to hug and kiss and celebrate with the man about to be my husband. On a day so often marked with schedules and timelines and frenzy, for a few short minutes everything came to a stop. It was just us. I'd never been more sure of anything. I'd made a thousand choices over the past twelve months to make our wedding day unforgettable, and this little moment of quiet reaffirmed choosing him was the best choice I'd ever made.

After the first look was done and the photos taken, when everyone's makeup had been touched up and ties straightened, Ben and I, our families, and the wedding party gathered in the house. We laughed together and prayed together and peered like children out the big bay windows of the kitchen, watching and waving as guests began to pour into the space surrounding the stone pool beside which we'd soon say our vows. When it was time for the ceremony to begin, Ben gave my hand a big squeeze, wished me good luck, and went to line up with the pastor and groomsmen.

I remember my heart pounding as I waited with Dad for everyone else to make their way down the aisle. I had never been more ready yet more overwhelmed, and I was acutely aware of the gravity of what this day meant. Love was no longer just a feeling Ben and I shared. It was now the single biggest choice and promise that we'd ever make to each other. A promise that I knew would feel easier and truer on some days than it did others, but one that I couldn't imagine waiting another second to make.

Romantic love often starts out as a feeling. It's exciting and captivating and fills you up in ways you seldom experience in other circumstances. You become emotionally and physically under the influence of a person who makes you feel alive in ways that few others ever will. For some this happens slowly, over years and years of pursuit and struggle and growth. For some, like Ben and me, it happens quickly.

The first time we met was actually the second time. The first time Ben and I met was just a year after graduating from college, and our exchange didn't go much beyond a hello and a few dances at our good friend Caroline's wedding. Apparently, I'd made more of an impression on him than he had on me because he swore he tried to get up the nerve to talk to me the day after. But the festivities came to a close, and I jetted back to California, where I was interning with a winery during the harvest season.

It would be more than two years until we met again on Caroline's back patio. Ben was now a second-year law student clerking for a judge in Nashville, and I was in the midst of opening my own restaurant in town. The meeting was equally as unexpected as it was unsuccessful. To him, it was the realization of a two-year desire to talk to me, but his eagerness caught me completely off guard. Without much of an introduction or a "Remember me, Mattie? It's Ben," he jumped away from the grill he was manning and right into my path as I headed inside for a snack.

"Hey, I've been thinking about it, and I'd really like to take you on a date."

That was it? Though I appreciated his wildly confident, straight-to-the-point approach, I didn't know Ben. It also didn't feel right saying yes when I had been casually seeing someone else. I knew nothing long-term would pan out with the other guy, but I was so surprised by Ben's question (and hungry for some queso) that I just brushed it off.

"I really can't," I replied as I moved toward the door. "I'm sorry."

"Why not?" he countered.

"Because I'm seeing someone." That should have been enough for him to let it go, but he took another step toward the door and attempted one more block. I felt like I was stuck in a scene from *The Notebook*. Just get off the Ferris wheel, Noah, geez!

"Well, when can I ask you again?"

If that wasn't the strangest thing I'd ever heard. *When can I ask you again?* As if he were happy to count down the days until my current relationship ended. I felt pretty sure it would end, eventually, but Ben didn't know that. It was such an arrogant yet oddly attractive question.

I'm pretty sure I laughed, sheerly out of shock, and then mumbled an arbitrary, "I don't know. In a month?"

And with that he left it alone, and I went about the party. Three months later, I got a text from an 865 number I didn't know: "Hey, Mattie. It's Ben Selecman. I asked you if I could take you out a few months ago at Caroline's, and you said to wait a month. I gave it a few extra for good measure. So how about that date?"

By this point the other guy and I had indeed fizzled out. I was so impressed with Ben's persistence, I thought, *Why not one date?*

A week or so later, Ben drove up to Nashville from Memphis (he was now back at law school) and took me out to dinner. We sat at the tiny bar of one of my favorite local restaurants, where he ordered a beer and, in the same breath, asked to bless our meal.

He was handsome and charming, so incredibly confident yet genuinely kind. Every time he thanked our server for something, Ben looked him in the eye and called him by name. I told him about my plan to open my own restaurant, and by his response, you'd think I'd offered him ownership in the company. He seemed more excited for my dream than I did a lot of days. From that day forward, he was my biggest cheerleader, always believing more in me than I even did in myself.

That evening, we talked about our families and our plans. We laughed and poked fun at each other as though we'd been friends for years. We shared our first meal and our first kiss. When the night was finished, he went back to school in Memphis, and I was left wondering, *How on earth did I miss this guy twice before?*

That was November 13, 2015, and we talked every day from then until our very last together.

Our relationship picked up with unexpected speed after that. I went down to visit him in Memphis and then spent our third date as his guest to his little brother's wedding. Yes, you read that correctly: I'd spent a total of two meals and a couple of weeks calling and texting with this guy before going as his date to his only sibling's wedding, where Ben was the best man. Even then I knew this was a little hasty, to say the least, but there was something about Ben that was already so familiar and safe. *Why not?* I thought. *Sink or swim, right?*

The wedding was a blast. I've never clicked so quickly with so many people. It was like looking months down the road and getting a sneak peek of his huge heart for his family and friends and his mantra to always live life to the fullest. If romantic love starts as a feeling, I was feeling it big time. I called my friend Lindsey on the drive home and expressed this exact thought in the most fumbled and sloppy and "I know this sounds crazy" way you can imagine. I didn't tell her I loved him or that I was going to marry him, but I think even then my heart knew what my head was scared to admit. He was *it* for me—my person, my equal, the love of my life.

Ten months later, after Ben had finished law school and decided to move to Nashville, we were engaged. I was totally surprised—and completely not. I'd known since date three this day would happen, though it came a little sooner than I expected. It felt fast, but why would we wait another day?

I know now the quick timing was one of God's greatest kindnesses to us. He put a fire and a fearlessness in our relationship that allowed us the most time we could have together as husband and wife before he took Ben away. I was ecstatic to be his wife, and after another year of planning and house searching and preparing, we were married.

At the white-rose-adorned altar behind my parents' home, I vowed to love Ben for the rest of my life. In that moment everything faded away. If you've been married, you may remember those few minutes in which all you can literally see is the face of the person who cherishes you and chose you. The world is still, and though you may be shaking (or, in Ben's case, swaying back and forth like a kid with uncontainable excitement), you have never felt so perfectly safe.

"I, Mattie, take thee, Ben, to be my wedded husband, to have and to hold from this day forward, for better, for worse, for richer, for poorer, in sickness and in health, to love and to cherish, 'til death do us part, according to God's holy ordinance; to you, I pledge my faith."

As we exchanged rings my mind raced with pictures and hopes and dreams of what those words might mean. Sure, they would mean hardship, as every marriage experiences, but they would also mean new adventures and greater trust and a shared life lived to the full. New trips to take and projects to tackle. Maybe a dog or two and at least three children. I knew, with time, tough days would come, but for now, we were just at the starting line.

The following months brought the deepest, surest, most un-wavering friendship I'd ever experienced. Ben made me kinder, and I made him more responsible. He pepped me up, and I calmed him down. We shared dreams and long drives and lots of laughter, and our porch and our table were always full. We loved in ways that felt rich beyond our years and youthful without the drama. We were as much different as we were alike, and our future looked the same, no matter which one of us painted the picture.

I'm convinced parts of Song of Solomon were written after that year of our marriage. Cookouts, long talks on the porch, hand-holding and winks across a crowd, new life. No, no babies, but a precious little Lab puppy who planted us deeper in love than we knew our young roots could reach. Bliss. Wholeness. Divinely appointed love, not void of real frustrations but buoyed by the vows that we'd made to each other and to the Lord.

Our first year of marriage was full of the beautiful parts of the promise "to have and to hold." Standing at the altar, I expected "bet-ter" and "richer" and "health," as every bride does. I expected to love and to cherish with death far, far off in the future. I didn't expect the second half of these promises to come true until much later in life.

If I'm honest, I didn't think much about them at all until they did come true.

FOR WORSE AND IN SICKNESS

For Labor Day weekend, Ben and I went to Palm Beach, Florida, with four other couples, among them my two sisters and their boy-friends. Four in our group, including Ben, had celebrated birthdays the week before, and we decided to enjoy the holiday at the beach. That Saturday morning, the girls walked by the ocean and lounged at the pool while Ben and his two best friends played golf together on the resort's stunning course. If he said it once that day, he said it at least twenty times: "Today's been the perfect day."

Later that evening we decided to take a dinner cruise on my dad's boat. We ate seafood and raised toasts and watched the sunset as we sailed down the Intracoastal Waterway, ending the night at a local beach bar for live music and dancing.

As the evening started to wind down, we had to take shelter under a small tiki hut to let a pop-up thunderstorm pass. When the rain stopped, we gathered our crew and headed back to the boat, ready to call it a night. Having reached the end of the dock, Ben hurried up the slippery steps to the boat to help some of the girls get up safely. But as his sandal hit the wet metal steps, he crashed back onto the concrete dock.

He didn't move. I raced over to his side, starting to panic but hoping the fall might leave him with just a mild concussion. He was unconscious for a moment, but then his eyes opened back up.

If not for the off-duty EMTs at the marina, we might not have called an ambulance. Ben was experiencing nothing more than some disorientation and a headache, the kind of effects anyone who had slipped and fallen might experience. I now know the extreme goodness and intentionality of the Lord in this moment, as these medically trained strangers not only encouraged me to take Ben to the ER immediately but also called and facilitated a quick ambulance pickup.

It was almost midnight by the time Ben received a CT scan at St. Mary's Medical Center. Between the exhaustion and the tears and being in a totally unfamiliar place, I hardly took in the details of what the ER doctor was explaining. But one word—*surgery*—shocked me back into reality. Because of the height he'd fallen from and the force of the impact, Ben's brain was starting to swell. It wasn't necessary to cut his skull open yet, the doctor told me, but it was likely to become so in the next twelve hours. What did I want to do?

What do I want to do? What I want to do is shut my eyes and go back to that boat and never get off. What I want to do is have you tell me what's best and not make me choose. What I want to do is wake up from this nightmare and have someone tell me it isn't real. Too fearful of what could happen during surgery, I decided to wait until it was absolutely necessary. Then I made the hardest two phone calls of my life.

I dreaded calling Ben's parents and mine, but I knew I had to. I explained to them as best I could what the surgeon had said and encouraged them to get a flight to Florida first thing in the morning. Never in a million years had I imagined making that call in the middle of night. Never had I expected to sit shivering overnight in an ICU chair, holding my husband's hand and hearing monitors beep, beep, beep without rest.

In the morning, Ben was still slightly awake. He was able to see me and tell me he loved me, though he continued to doze in and out and was clearly in pain despite the medicine. His parents arrived in time to sit and talk with him, another merciful hand dealt from the Lord. But in the middle of the following night, I got a call from the neurosurgeon, expressing that an immediate craniotomy was crucial to Ben's maintaining full brain function. If the swelling got too bad, he could lose his personality, judgment, maybe even motor function.

After the surgery, which proved successful in the short run, Ben remained in a medically induced coma for eleven days. I would have given anything to be where he was. To take the ventilator out of his throat and the EEG wires off of his stapled scalp. To make all the monitors and the beeping and the IVs go away. To squeeze his hand and feel him squeeze mine back, just one more time. To take his place.

For those eleven days he lay poked, stapled, and unconscious, his body mechanically operated down to the tiniest detail by ICU staff. Some days I prayed and reminded Ben he held the same eternal inheritance as Jesus and the saints. Some days I blabbed on and talked to him as if we were sharing Jet's Pizza together and watching college football. Some days I played George Jones and Merle Haggard and clips from our favorite movie, *Sweet Home Alabama*. Those things—the intimate, uninteresting-to-anyone-else-in-the-world things—sustained me. They made us still *us*, not just a man in a coma and a woman with his last name. They brought life to the long days of not knowing what would happen. Long days of living in worse and in sickness. Long days that were haunted and teased, moment by moment, by the possibility that death really could do us part.

When trauma strikes, love goes from being a feeling to being a choice, in huge, physical, real ways. Every morning, I had to choose to be brave. I had to choose to hope, even though I had no assurance how this situation would end. Every morning I felt as though I were dressing for a strange battle, walking into a war zone on foreign terrain with prayer as my only weapon. But I knew I had to keep choosing love. Choosing to love Ben in a coma, not knowing what kind of mental deficits he could wake up with, without promise that he'd be the same kind, generous, charismatic man I married. And choosing to love a God who, though I trusted him, still allowed Ben's body to break down and suffer multiple strokes that, in the blink of a moment, rendered him brain-dead.

That's a word no one imagines they'll have to hear: *brain-dead*. Even when I did hear it, I didn't believe it was true. After the doctors explained to us the "options," which are not options at all, I still felt sure God would fix Ben. I spent nearly four hours on the cold hospital floor, praying and begging and claiming with confidence that Ben was about to be a miracle. I knew God could save him. But when the final MRI came back with even more neurological damage than the previous ones, I started to feel like the fight might be over.

At the end of the day—which had felt like more than forty days in one—our families and I returned to the hotel for the night. At this point Ben's body was being run entirely by machines, and I was running on empty. I had no idea how to choose to take him off life support, and I honestly didn't know if I could forgive myself if I did. All I could do was keep holding out hope for a miracle.

But in the middle of the night, around two o'clock, I jumped up to a call from the hospital with news that Ben's heart was failing. If we could get there quickly, the doctors could keep him alive so we could say goodbye.

I'd never understood the term *out-of-body experience* until that moment. I didn't know you could feel so acutely aware of every pain and every hurt and also feel utterly in shock at the same time.

I didn't know that love could physically hurt until I watched mine slip away. I didn't know you could feel supernaturally surrounded by God and feel abandoned by him in the same moment.

At the hospital, I signed the papers that I, as his wife, had to sign. Before the nurse on shift that night pulled the ventilator from Ben's throat, she told us his passing could be quick. Even as his chest stopped moving and his lips fell open, I couldn't take my hand from his. I couldn't walk away from the man I'd promised to love forever. I couldn't help but lay on his chest and pull his mouth to mine like I had so many times before.

"'Til death do us part" rang through my whole being, a cruel chorus of a nightmare just come true. A promise cut off. I had nothing to say. Those words said it all.

LEMONS ON FRIDAY

Within hours of Ben's final breaths, waves of condolences and prayers flooded my phone. I had the capacity to read, much less reply to, very few. I sat on the hotel balcony, frozen like a frame from a horrible movie: blank faced, empty, staring. My Bible sat next to me, tearstained and closed. I'd clutched it, clung to it, and carried it around every inch of the hospital those past weeks, never believing it might not hold up its end of the bargain.

"The Word was with God, and the Word was God" (John 1:1). That Word seemed silent now. What about God's promises and his faithfulness and his power to heal? What about ask and you shall receive? Why had God chosen to hush his powers while the man he'd gifted me was so wrongfully taken away?

Silence.

And, truthfully, that's what I wanted in that moment. I wanted silence from God. As far as I could tell, he'd been silent for twelve days when I thought he was working. Why should he start talking now?

Then my phone rang. On the screen I saw that the call was from Ben's cousin J. B. Selecman, who had married us the year before. When I answered, I could hardly get out a hello.

In his deep East Tennessee accent, I heard J. B. say simply, "We love you, buddy. We've been praying all night."

No *I'm sorry*, no *how are you doing?* No questions that didn't have answers but that people ask anyway. Just love and prayer.

Right before we hung up, J. B. reminded me that Ben had just won the greatest victory anyone could imagine. He gave me a place to go in the book I'd so soundly shut, a promise in which to trust, and a reminder of the Savior with whom Ben was celebrating at that very moment in heaven. In his quick phone call, he turned my eyes off of all I'd just lost and refocused them on all Ben had just gained.

He led me here, to the passage he would preach with elation and thanksgiving at Ben's funeral a few days later:

When the perishable has been clothed with the imperishable,
and the mortal with immortality, then the saying that is written
will come true: "Death has been swallowed up in victory."

"Where, O death, is your victory?
Where, O death, is your sting?"
(1 Corinthians 15:54–55 NIV)

This promise has been my lifeline, my manna in the desert. On my darkest days, I strain to refocus on Ben's elation in eternity more than on my pain here without him. Praise Jesus that the same moment I saw my beloved take his last earthly breath, Ben took his first heavenly breath and saw his beloved Savior. I would never have survived without this truth, this promise from God that, unlike our earthly vows, can never be cut off.

I hate that my marriage vows only lasted forty-nine weeks. But experiencing the worse, the sickness, and the death they included doesn't negate the better, the health, the love and cherishing that came with them. No one acknowledges the bitter parts of this promise as they take their wedding vows, but most everyone will experience them at some point. My point just came too soon.

And like these promises we made on our wedding day, many of God's vows to us include promises for suffering that we overlook until we can't. Not until I lost Ben did I begin to hear the *true* pulse that beats at the heart of God's Word. The fine print inked between the lines of what we long to be a cozy prosperity gospel but is, in fact, just the opposite. If we really walked with Moses and Abraham, Job and Paul, we would tread a path laced with thorns, charted with hardship and sorrow:

> Consider it pure joy, my brothers and sisters, whenever you face trials of many kinds . . . (James 1:2 NIV)

> "In this world you will have trouble. . . ." (John 16:33 NIV)

> Just as the sufferings of Christ overflow to us . . . (2 Corinthians 1:5 CSB)

> There was given to me a thorn in the flesh, a messenger of Satan to torment me . . . (2 Corinthians 12:7 NASB)

I'm starting to see that the real subtitle of the Bible is "Lemons on Friday." But we never lead with these promises for suffering. We never start with the agony of crucifixion Friday but with the glory of resurrection Sunday. We do all we can to not live our lives in the fear of Friday or Saturday but to hoard, herald, and hold captive the joy of Sunday. Why wouldn't we? We long for Sunday just as we long for lemonade.

Sour lemons, suffering, and death aren't much of a sales pitch to follow Christ. "Come hurt with us! Come bear the broken world's bullets with us!" These are words you'll never see on the church's marquee sign. But the truth is, in vain attempts to evangelize and convert, we've diluted the gospel into sugar water for the sake of the Great Commission. In trying to pacify our doubts and bolster our broken hearts, we hold tight to the promises' victorious endings but hush their assurance of painful beginnings.

That is, until life gives us lemons—the bitter, stomach-turning, smile-stealing lemons that Scripture reveals over and over again in the lives of its most celebrated saints.

This is where we doubt God's goodness, isn't it? In our times of ravenous need, he sits on his throne and watches us grimace while we eat lemons. Our deepest desire is for him to take them away, to give us a single bite of something sweet. We hurt and we wonder, *Did God plan for our pain, or did he sit back and allow it?* Neither picture shows much of a loving, good God, does it? Don't funerals of twenty-eight-year-old husbands give legitimate cause for the universal cry, *With all this suffering, how can God be good?*

I wish I had a foolproof, pastor-approved answer to that question, both for your sake and mine. I don't. What I can tell you is that in the middle of my worst nightmare come true, even when I didn't know how to talk to God or trust God, God continued to

We long
for Sunday
just as we
long for
lemonade.

_____

show me he was good. Somehow, in those first days especially, I physically felt God being good to me in ways that far exceeded a theological explanation. Prayer was no longer a one-way dialogue; it was a palpable, protective presence. Song was no longer mindless worship; it was the melodic cry of emotional chaos I couldn't explain. Nature was no longer an inanimate backdrop; it sat with me like a friend. Even in the literal valley of the shadow of death, the Lord continued to breathe life into me in ways only he can.

Life in a broken world where everyone will face suffering is full of lemons on Friday. Full of outcomes we don't expect and heartbreaks we won't get explanations for. The Bible warns us of this. We just choose to see the "for better" side of its promises until we're forced to see the "for worse."

My hope, and our greatest hope as humans who will inevitably face loss, is that just as Christ promises believers bitter lemons and sorrowful Fridays, so, too, does he promise us lemonade on Sunday. He has already gifted us eternal victory. He has conquered all the sin, sorrow, and death we face. While the beginnings of these painful promises for trial are inevitable, the good news triumphs at their sentences' end:

> . . . because you know that the testing of your faith produces perseverance. Let perseverance finish its work so that you may be mature and complete, not lacking anything. (James 1:3–4 NIV)

> ". . . But take heart! I have overcome the world." (John 16:33 NIV)

> . . . so also through Christ our comfort overflows. If we are afflicted, it is for your comfort and salvation. If we are comforted, it is for your comfort, which produces in you patient endurance

of the same sufferings that we suffer. And our hope for you is firm, because we know that as you share in the sufferings, so you will also share in the comfort. (2 Corinthians 1:5–7 csb)

. . . Three times I pleaded with the Lord to take it away from me. But he said to me, "My grace is sufficient for you, for my power is made perfect in weakness." (2 Corinthians 12:8–9 niv)

God grieves this broken world and all the ways it shatters our happiness and assaults our hope. And he warns us! He tells us we will face a life filled with lemons on Friday. You and I are living in the middle of these promises, day in and day out. In the middle of the already-but-not-yet of being saved and adopted through Christ while still being subject to sorrow in this world.

Nothing about the pretty parts of my wedding vows made the painful parts easier. But I still celebrate them because they're still real. I pray you can learn to do the same with God's promises to us, both the promise for suffering and the promise that he has conquered pain, sorrow, and death forever. I hope you savor the merciful foretastes of his protection, presence, and peace that can transcend your deepest wounds here on earth. And on the hardest days, I pray you can cling to the truth of God's overwhelming love for you, even as you face Fridays full of lemons.

two

PUMPKINS AND PORCHES

WHAT DO I DO NOW?

The LORD will fight for you;
you need only to be still.

EXODUS 14:14 NIV

Not until I lost Ben did I consider how cruel the timeline is between someone's death and their burial. The plans and the choices those left behind must endure on top of their shock and mourning come on brutally fast. The decisions are endless. Choosing the flowers, the casket, the music, the location. Picking out photos to show, clothes to wear, scriptures to read. Who will speak at the service? Who will be the pallbearers? Who will take us to the gravesite? There are a thousand tasks and very little time, and not a part of you wants to do any of it.

But the whirlwind is partially a blessing, too, I think. The few days between Ben's death and his service forced me to immediately be active. And when I was busy, I didn't have to sit with the unfathomable truth that my husband was gone. It's always been easier for me to *do* in spite of feelings than to sit in the middle of them. So the decisions—the doing—helped shield me from the full impact of a life so suddenly in shambles.

That whole week still feels completely surreal, like a strange dream that I floated in and out of and somehow eventually woke up from. But unlike the nightmares we experience in our sleep and find relief from when we wake, this nightmare was real. And waking up made things feel anything but better.

We held Ben's service and burial five days after he died, and I delivered his eulogy. I sat with our families in what our church calls "the window room" as guests entered the sanctuary. Through the sprawling window, we could see them, but they couldn't see us. We watched them file in just as we had watched the arriving guests through the kitchen windows on Ben's and my wedding day a year before. Hundreds of people filed in, many under the age of thirty. Besides a prayer together, we sat silent. I felt as though we were a strange troop of weary soldiers about to go into battle, and I was the idiot who'd volunteered to stand on the front line. To stand up on behalf of my husband and our family and somehow utter words that attempted to honor him and offered the slightest bit of condolence for everyone piling into those pews.

I knew I wasn't ready, but I also had an unexplainable calm. Giving the eulogy felt like an assignment, something I hadn't volunteered for but had been commissioned to do.

The day Ben died, while on my flight home from Florida, the Lord gave me everything he wanted me to say in the eulogy. While the rest of our family slept, no doubt exhausted from almost two weeks of hoping and waiting and weeping, I typed into my phone every word the Holy Spirit was downloading into my mind.

So on September 17, after the first hymn was played, I took the stage in front of a packed sanctuary. I looked down at the floor from the podium and thought that Ben would have liked the cowhide rug on the stage. I reminded myself not to look anyone in the eye. If I did, I knew I wouldn't make it through. At multiple points, I paused and thought, *Is this real? How did I get here?*

But in spite of how scary and surreal it was, I felt peace. Saying those words on that stage was exactly where I was supposed to be, even though I didn't want to be there. I trusted God's goodness to deliver me through this terrifying assignment. He gave me the same message the day of the funeral as he did when he told me to write this book: I didn't have to say anything perfectly; I just had to be honest about our story and honest about who God is. If I answered this overwhelming call to show up, he would jump in and do the rest.

I read every word straight from my phone, my voice and hands shaking and eyes blinking rapidly in an attempt to bat away tears. But I did what God had called me to do. I showed up, and I told the truth about love—mine for Ben, and the Lord's for all of us.

And in this raw, painful, surreal delivery of my husband's eulogy, the Lord revealed to me that the great moments he uses for our good and his glory come not when we're strong but when we're weak beyond imagination. He put me on the stage but put himself in the spotlight. I was on the mic, but the words shared were his. I was simply the supporting actress speaking from a divine script.

Kind friends praised me for my courage that day, but I knew the strength was also not my own. I knew God had called me to that stage so that in the very first moments of my grief, I would be reminded of the miraculous power to which I have access when I simply fix my eyes on him. It was then that I understood all God would ask me to do moving forward is to show up in the chaos and let him work. He has been faithful to strengthen and sustain me through unimaginable pain because, with God, absolutely nothing is impossible (Philippians 4:13).

Then came the weeks following the service and burial, when most family and friends had gone home. This time felt like a terrible time warp. I felt as though I'd settled into a strange new reality. An unknown place, ringing, *What now? What now?* Of course, there is no clear or easy answer to that question, but I longed for something else to do. Something to keep my hands busy enough that I could ignore my destroyed heart a little longer. Life had come to a screeching halt. Grief stopped everything, and I had nowhere to run. I was stagnant and stuck and, all of a sudden, without distractions.

I wanted to know what to do to make the pain less, to make myself heal quicker. But grief cripples us—our minds, our motivations, our ability to reason. We know we're lost, but where is a map? Is there a map? Grief often leaves us feeling helpless because the only way to navigate grief is to quit trying to navigate it at all. Life chooses for us *when* we are to grieve, not *if* we grieve, because we all will. But when the option to navigate, to do, to fix is ripped from our control, our only hope is that with time and with Christ, we can find some new bearings.

But in the meantime, what would my day-to-day look like? As I waited on the Lord and waited for a time when joy could reign again, what would I do? If I wallowed in bed and fasted because I didn't have energy to walk to the kitchen, I'd be pitied. If I numbed and distracted and denied, I'd be avoiding. If I worked and smiled and laughed because it felt good to do so, I'd be hard-hearted. If I drank without stopping or prayed without ceasing, I'd be escaping. So what was I to do?

I realized quickly that all I really wanted from friends and family was for them to show up so that I wasn't doing the day alone. I needed them to be with me. In the same way, I needed to be present for myself. I needed to show up for me. Showing up can be accepting help with laundry or with your dog or with kids if you have them. It can be taking a shower or taking a walk down your street when the only place you want to go is back to bed. It can be putting on real pants or enjoying a good meal instead of reaching for another sugary snack. Often it is telling your people honestly what you need and reminding yourself that you're not a burden to them. They love you. They want to show up for you too.

Showing up in the small things is powerful. In the very early days of grief, I needed daily reminders that though it was hard to believe in the moment, I really would survive. Showing up is how I resisted shutting down.

We must simply show up—whatever that means on any particular day. Besides help around the house, prayers for peace, and gracious dinner deliveries, isn't the act of showing up all we want from others? Why not hold ourselves to the same standard?

And when we show up, God shows up too. Every time. He shows up in rainbows and gentle breezes, in words of friends and laughter-inducing old stories. He shows up with supernatural peace and a slow drip of adrenaline that, though we may still be in shock, mercifully sweeps us from one day to the next.

This is all we can do at first: let God carry us through whatever the twenty-four hours in front of us might bring. Each day I strained to get out of bed and show up—with God, with a friend, with whatever and whoever was before me—I became a little more confident that I could do it again the next day. Maybe one day showing up wouldn't be such a struggle. Maybe one day it would be second nature again.

SORTING PUMPKINS

One sunny morning in October, showing up led to a new step, a new something to do in the midst of my grief. This time it meant not just being present but actually being active. It meant creating.

On a Wednesday just three weeks after the funeral, my best friend, Emily, pitched me a silly and exhausting idea. That day she was my keeper, the term I jokingly used to refer to whoever was on the Excel sheet tasked with not leaving me alone. A true southern girl, she may as well have been oozing pumpkin spice latte from her pores when she suggested we go to a pumpkin patch and get me some fall decor.

I should preface this story by saying that I buy only fake plants because I always kill the real ones, and my idea of decor is collector wine bottles, copies of classic novels, and taxidermy against an all-white, fairly seasonless landscape. I could barely keep myself alive at this point, and the thought of large, heavy produce that would eventually rot on my front porch before I got around to throwing it out wasn't extraordinarily appealing.

But I could tell this was Emily's sincere step toward showing up for me. I knew even then how helpless she and all my people felt and how desperately they wanted to cheer me up or distract me, if

This is all we
can do at first:
let God carry us
through whatever
the twenty-four
hours in front of
us might bring.

———

even for a little while. And for Em, doing so involved pumpkins. So I showed up, and off we went to the pumpkin patch.

I'd never realized there were so many different kinds of pumpkins. Different shapes and colors and sizes. Some seemed meant for carving and some were twisted and bumpy, like they were covered in warts. I still wasn't feeling incredibly into this activity, but it was nice to have my mind on something else for a while. After an hour or so of lugging around and filling our Lowe's wagons full of gourds, we wrapped up our little outing.

I went home that day with eight pumpkins and a sense of peace no part of me had expected to find. I felt content, yet, at the same time, something stirred deep within in a way it hadn't since the moment Ben died. I felt energy again—and actual excitement to go put those dang pumpkins out on my front steps. Maybe I thought passersby would see the seasonal setup and assume a happy family still lived inside. Maybe there was a sense of restored control over something as trivial as fall decor that removed me for a moment from my reality. Or maybe I felt energized simply because I had the courage to show up and remind myself that I could still make beauty from something so plain. And if that were true, maybe God really could make beauty out of all my pain.

I believe there is tremendous power in small, creative acts. I went outside and used my hands, my eyes, and my imagination to compile something beautiful from materials so simple and unremarkable. I felt control and gratification and productivity and purpose.

This moment shed light on a crucial truth for me as I faced the daunting times ahead. Many days the best we can do is show up and be with God and our people. Celebrate those days because they are brave. But on the days we feel extra brave, on the days the Emilys in our lives take gentle steps to remind us we're still very much capable and alive, small acts of creation become like cortisone shots for our souls. They jolt us back into feeling as if we can establish some beauty and goodness in our lives, in our own ways. And each of us will find that creativity and vitality at our own paces, in our own spaces.

Cooking also became a life-giving outlet for me. The day of our visit to the pumpkin patch was the first day I'd cooked anything since Ben died, and that act, too, brought an odd sense of both tranquility and energy. There was something intrinsically peaceful about bringing delicious order out of uncooked chaos. That day I also started journaling to process the overwhelming pain that I was afraid to face head-on. My journal became not just a release valve but also a crucial tool in my overall restoration. It was the starting point and inspiration for nearly everything between these pages.

When you feel helpless in your sorrow, I encourage you to take some small steps to create. Search with supportive friends in tow for everyday activities that will sneakily bring back life. The more I heal and move forward, the more I'm realizing God doesn't just meet us in the big things, in the eulogy moments. I'm seeing him meet me all the more tenderly in the small things, in the pumpkin patch.

This, dear friends, is perseverance: moving forward little by little, moment by moment, until another tomorrow comes. And remember as you cook or write or sort pumpkins, creating and ordering and shaping, God is doing the same thing with your mess. Everything that fell out of place when Ben died, the Lord was holding and hauling and arranging into something beautiful— even though at the time, I couldn't see anything but the rotted pieces. Paul's words to the Romans on suffering may bring us encouragement today, as they remind us that the Lord can always repurpose our ashes for beauty if we let him.

> Not only that, but we rejoice in our sufferings, knowing that suffering produces endurance, and endurance produces character, and character produces hope. (Romans 5:3–4)

Hope is on the horizon, friends. You simply need to show up and keep your eyes open to see the beauty the Lord is creating in you.

A PLACE TO REST

But what of the countless days when we feel we can't persevere? What about the days we're running on empty and literally cannot show up?

Then, we must rest.

Isn't that the universal prescription for viruses, food poisoning, mild injuries? Antibiotics or pain meds can be issued, but they are always accompanied by the instructive, "Just rest!" And so we do, most of the time feeling our attempts to rest are in vain. We watch reruns and sip orange Gatorade and flat Sprite while the rest of our healthy friends whine about being at work or school. After a while of resting, of feeling achy and stagnant and burdensome to people, we'd love to be at work!

Mono always seemed the worst to me. It creeps in mercilessly with virtually no symptoms and then debilitates you on a dime. It's also not a twenty-four- or forty-eight-hour thing. There's nothing about mono that's brief. The same is true of grief. Even in cases where a loved one's death is expected, the weight of grief comes on in an instant. Until their passing, there is hope in spite of the knowledge of what might come, but then at the moment they go, there's immediate emptiness. It's emotional mono.

What does it mean to rest in the midst of life-altering tragedy? When the sickness of the heart that plagues us is chronic but not fatal, when the future we longed for is also buried and gone, how do we rest?

And if we do rest, does that mean we're accepting our awful circumstances? Do we have to quiet the anger, questions, and desperate clutching for some sort of understanding? Does resting mean waving a white flag?

The world's answer is, "No, you're stronger than you think—just keep fighting."

My wounded soul's answer is, "Hell no, none of this is fair! This should never have happened to me."

The Lord's answer is, "Yes, because I love you."

What's beautiful about the biblical concept of rest is that it takes the load off of us. In Greek the word *katapausis* describes this idea of rest: "a resting place."[1] It isn't only a verb; it's also a noun. *Katapausis* is a spiritual and emotional position we call on God to place us into, not one that we are left to find or achieve on our own. It is a place where, though our circumstances may not be still, our souls are. While our stories may feel hopeless, our spirits are given permission to hope again. It's a place where we feel steady and secure and rooted in the moment because we can feel God's kindness as he quiets our hurt and anxiety, even if just for a little while. While moments of rest do not eliminate our hurt, for a time there is a little peace to accompany all the pain. It's an invitation to simply be where you are, to remember how incredibly loved by God you are, and to hit pause on the suffering pressing in.

Sometimes rest looks just like we usually picture it, like solitude or quiet or physical stillness. Looking back, I think one of my first real moments of rest came on a regular night, sitting on my back porch with my friend Alyson. We weren't doing anything special. She, like Emily had been before, was my keeper that day. She'd picked me up to go get sushi and then offered to stay until I went to bed. For a while we listened to songs from one of our favorite country artists, Eric Church. But after the first round of that record had run its course, I remember her asking me one simple question: What could she do for me?

I knew she, too, felt at a loss as to how to help. I could tell she didn't want to overstep, but at the same time, she longed to do something to bring me a little lightness.

All I knew to tell her was, "I don't know what I need, Al. But when I do, I'll let you know." And that was the truth. Because grief arrests our minds and our thinking, we often don't know how to answer the kind questions people ask. And that's okay. Often the truest answer is, "Just be with me." I knew I didn't want to sit in that night's silence alone, and the Lord knew above all else, more than distractions or encouraging words, I needed rest. I needed to sit still in the quiet with a friend who loved me and with a God who never intended for me to bear life's burdens on my own.

I can't tell you anything else we talked about after that or whether we talked at all. But the Lord taught me in that moment the power of simply being alongside another person. Of being with someone who loves you and who is willing to ask the hard questions or sit in the hard silence so that your emptiness has time to be refilled. Rest comes just as much in community as it does in solitude. It took me a while and some prideful "I'm fines" before I let the people in my life love and care for me completely, but what a glorious witness to how God loves his children through his other children. Let your people in. Let them be God's hands for you. Let them help you rest.

Make no mistake: rest is not a quick fix. It's not a cure. I still cried when I went to bed that night, and I still needed rest again the next day. But in a holy place of rest, the Lord slowly and meticulously brings back life, not by eliminating sorrow but by empowering peace to overcome it; by meeting fruitless coping mechanisms with faithful community; and by filling emptiness in loss back to fullness in Christ.

Whether we find rest with loved ones or in personal moments of solitude, rest is a vital part of our healing. It is the place where the Lord restores our strength and fills up our empty tanks so that we can continue to show up and create and find life again. The Lord will place you into a position of rest and peace even in the midst of your most unimaginable pain. All you have to do is show up and ask him to. I assure you with absolute confidence, he will.

But even with this call to rest, let us not deny the pain, numb the broken heart, or ignore the mono. Let us praise Jesus that, in him, we can show up through the sickness, create in the chaos, and find true rest knowing that our sorrow is in his hands.

When we suffer traumatic loss or change, we're not expected to know what to do. There aren't steps or tricks to build back up to a new "normal." The Lord doesn't need us to have a game plan. He just wants us to show up. He wants our trust. He wants to lavish us with hope that doesn't make sense in the midst of suffering. And as his tears fall for our pain, his greatest desire is for our pain to find rest in his power. For us to call on his name, crawl into his arms, and take a seat as he begins to create something new and beautiful.

three

FIRST STEPS

WILL I ALWAYS HURT THIS MUCH?

> We are afflicted in every way, but not
> crushed; perplexed, but not driven to
> despair; persecuted, but not forsaken;
> struck down, but not destroyed.
>
> 2 CORINTHIANS 4:8–9

After any sort of sudden setback or loss, there is a period where the most courageous things we can do are to show up and to rest. We need this time! Time to process and lament and lend our energy to accepting whatever it is we don't want to accept. Time to just *be*—with our hurt, with our people, with our God—and not *do*. But eventually, we're faced with the grueling fact that we're going to have to move. In spite of the overwhelming pain, life won't always be on pause.

No matter what you've lost—a marriage, a child, a physical ability—the pain of an intimate part of your life being cut off isn't something that just goes away. It feels permanent because it is. It feels, in many ways, like an amputation—an aggressive, premature ending that leaves you the same person, in the same skin, but now having to navigate life without a limb. What we've lost is part of the fabric of who we are, and yet we have to learn how to be us without it. We have to learn to walk again.

In the first weeks after Ben's death, I had no interest in walking at all. No interest in working, no interest in leaving the house or doing anything that reemphasized I'd never move through life the same way again. Being still meant I didn't have to deal with Ben's things. It meant I didn't have to see or talk to people outside my circle who didn't know what to say. It meant I didn't have to reply to cards and letters and texts. I felt like my leg—part of the very foundation of who I am—had been cut off without explanation, and now I was expected to walk. But I had no idea *how*. So I stayed still. Maybe if I stayed still, I could just keep being Mattie and not have to be a widow.

Then a month or so passed, and being still wasn't helping me anymore. Reality began to set in, and I knew I was going to have to move. So I started to hobble. Sometimes it felt bearable, like when I made a trip to the grocery store or took a cycling class in the dark where my tears just looked like sweat. But most of the time it felt overwhelming and awkward. Like when I'd run into someone I knew who, of course, knew about what had happened. They'd say hello, then hesitate, clearly considering whether to mention it or pretend they didn't know. Which was worse? I preferred the pretending.

These interactions, the ones when I felt I could never erase the widow stamp from my forehead, hurt the most. They left me wondering not only if the pain would ever go away but also if it would always hurt this bad. Would it ever let up? At my very worst I even had moments of wishing the leg, the marriage, had never been there to begin with. At least it would hurt less that way.

You see, once I started to move again, I really felt the depth of the pain. Minutes alone felt like hours, one task felt like ten, and every time I saw a sunset, it meant the coming of another night without Ben. The adrenaline was gone, and the anger, fear, and fragility set in. These are our natural, human reactions to such an abrupt amputation, and they rear their ugly heads in our most feeble attempts to walk. We become angry because it's unfair, fearful because it's unfamiliar, and fragile because the pain stabs from so many directions that we don't know how to ask for help.

This is when I became tempted with placebos—unhealthy ways of numbing the pain. I'd kept myself still, deceivingly safe, and had resisted any forward motion. But with motion comes discomfort, and with discomfort often comes the temptation to numb.

Numbing is a natural reaction to pain, and placebos are everywhere. For some they look like overuse of drugs and alcohol. For some sex and physical pleasure become their anesthesia. But for most of us, the placebos are more subtle and less destructive. Overeating, overworking, binge-watching Netflix for days and days on end. Throwing ourselves intrusively into our kids' or parents' or friends' lives so we don't have to deal with our own. These placebos may not destroy us, but they are still just that: placebos—empty attempts to fix with sugar what only real medicine can heal.

No matter what we face—loss, depression, anxiety, fear, physical pain—we long to temper discomfort in any way we can.

We're all wired with an aversion to pain, but our means of subverting it show up in countless different ways. Some are avoidant; some are addictive; some are good and healthy.

Only the healthy approaches to addressing pain will actually bring healing. As in physical therapy, these approaches pinpoint the pain, push the spot that hurts, and build it back into function. They don't numb the pain; they help release it. But they're not the kind we generally reach for first. We don't want to walk because it hurts, so we reach for the placebos that give the impression of healing but, in reality, just postpone it and prolong the injury.

Everyone has different placebos, and it took me a while to identify mine and wean myself off of them. To realize that temporarily numbing to keep from falling apart wasn't really strength, as everyone praised me for, but weakness. Where they saw fight, I felt like I was putting up a front. Where they saw resilience, I saw running as fast as I could from emotion. Few of us invite suffering in well. Resisting it is natural. But being numb doesn't make us strong; it just slows down real healing.

So eventually I chucked the placebos. I addressed the nub. I told God I was weak and scared. I thanked him that his plan was good and said if he would help carry me, I was ready to try to walk. And it hurt like hell. All forward motion came with exhaustion, and any joy he granted was inevitably coupled with pain. But for the first time, there were moments of joy.

TALK ABOUT IT

I've now been on an over-three-year journey of emotional rehab. I've taken thousands of new steps, each of which hurt in unique ways.

The very first step for me was talking about my loss—not only with my loved ones or inner circle but with people I didn't know or hadn't seen in a while. People who couldn't know how to hold my grief or hear my story. People who I felt I needed to act okay around because I wasn't sure what they'd do if I fell apart.

It was mid-November, just two months after Ben's death, and the company I co-own was having a holiday pop-up shop at a local Nashville boutique. My amputation still felt extremely raw, and I'd kept mostly to myself and my inner circle of family and friends up to this point. But our company, NaSHEville, which we began building after closing my restaurant in June and before Ben's accident in September, was still very new, and after several weeks of laying low, I felt obligated to help out. The few followers we had knew about my story, as serving and advocating for widows is one of our missions, but we were just beginning to grow, so I wasn't too worried about having to talk about Ben.

So there I was, chatting with customers, selling T-shirts, and pretending to have two legs. I almost felt normal in the swing of working and playing the part of business owner. Then a young woman around my age approached. I launched into my spiel about who we are and what we do, but she cut me off mid-pitch.

"You're Mattie, right?"

"Yeah!" I said. "I'm one of the cofounders. How do you know about NaSHEville?"

Then she dropped the bomb: "I lost my husband too."

I was stunned, ripped instantly out of my pretend comfort zone and back into hobbling widow zone. *Why is this happening? Am I now the ambassador for all young widows? Why does this have to be me?*

Honestly, my gut impulse was to say, "I'm so sorry," and move on, acting too busy to talk. But as I stepped back and took a breath, it became glaringly obvious this was not a cruel coincidence. This was a chance to take a step.

Riddled with fear and vulnerability and uncertainty, I leaned out to give this stranger a hug. "I'm so sorry," I uttered—not to dismiss but to invite someone in who, if she was anything like me, had felt like the only woman in the world under thirty hurting the way I was hurting. Everyone in my inner circle loved me and sat with me and encouraged me, but none of them knew what the gaping hole in my chest felt like. None of them knew how cold my bed felt at night and how I sometimes wished I wouldn't wake up in the morning, but this woman did. And after ten minutes of conversation with Hailey, I felt for the first time that I truly wasn't alone. Like this tragedy really did happen to women who weren't sixty or seventy or eighty, and that there were others like me whose marriages were taken before they had ever really started.

My conversation with Hailey that day debunked the lie that I was the only one facing the sorrow I was facing. The small step to talk about my story with a stranger released a tiny bit of the pain. I might always hurt, but I didn't have to hurt alone. Sometimes the bravest thing we can do is talk honestly about our pain with someone who's lost the same leg, whether we know them or not.

Since that divine meeting, I've sat with countless women of every age who've been widowed. I've sat with moms who've lost children and friends who've lost parents. And though each time in those conversations my heart physically aches for Ben, I walk away more hopeful and reassured that it won't always hurt as badly as it does right now.

These first ventures back into reality, the moments of leaning into the hurt instead of numbing it, are excruciating. They are honest. They are brave. They are healing. They are exhausting. But please, friends, don't hide from them. Grieving takes courage, and most of the time, that courage comes in very small doses. Talking about the hurt, letting yourself feel the grief instead of avoiding or numbing—these things are warm-up stretches for our souls. They are the first bits of rehab for our hearts so that each new step forward becomes a little less painful.

PAIN AND JOY: THE BOTH-AND

With time and faith and boldness, I started to make actual strides. They were small strides, but I was moving back into some familiar rhythms Ben had been a part of.

One came by way of a TV series. While certainly not the most profound or spiritual way to engage my grief, it was one that opened my eyes to the *both-and* of life after loss: the paradox that suffering can be both painful and joyful at the same time.

During our first year of marriage, Ben and I had eagerly followed the first season of a modern western drama called *Yellowstone*. It was everything he loved—cowboys, farm life, and sweeping Montana landscapes. He would have left the city in a heartbeat to live that kind of life. The show hit the mark for me in a lot of ways, too, but mostly I loved that he loved it.

Several months after Ben died, the show's second season was released. I wasn't aware until Emily texted about it one day.

"Yellowstone, season 2!" she sent with a cowboy emoji. "Want to come watch?"

Though this invitation may seem trivial—*What's the big deal about going to watch a TV show?*—to me, it was such a kindness. A loving friend had reached out a hand and offered to face something with me that reminded me in yet another way I was alone. But even if I was alone, I didn't have to be alone by myself. Over the next several weeks, Emily made it a weekly appointment for her and her husband to sit with me in an hour-long space that, of course, made the Ben-shaped hole feel bigger but also allowed me to remember his presence in a small way that actually made me smile.

I experienced the same *both-and* of pain and joy during a "Friendsgiving" dinner with Ben's closest three friends and their wives. The six of them have since become my safe place on particularly painful days. There is something powerful and personal and almost protective about being around these people who loved Ben before they ever loved me. It's as if being with them allows me to take his spot. It lets me remember him in even more detail, with louder laughs and bigger hugs, because I know that's exactly how these friends remember him too.

But as much as I feel Ben's presence with our closest friends, those spaces also make it glaringly obvious that he's missing. In the places where I feel him the most present, I miss him the most. This is the awkward, uncomfortable, but redemptive rhythm of learning to walk again. And though it ushers in small moments of joy, it is still painful. Absolutely raw. Absolutely against everything I wanted healing to be.

Why do the few moments when I feel steady, secure, and unexpectedly joyful have to hurt the most? When I try to feel closest to Ben and to the people, places, and things he loved, why do I feel the deepest aches? For a long time, I wondered if I'd ever feel pure joy without looming clouds of pain again. I wondered if I would ever, ever stop hurting.

The truth is, I won't—not completely. And likely neither will you, regardless of what you're grieving. But the joy does come back.

It does come alongside the pain, and eventually, the pain isn't the only voice in the room.

Trust me, leaning into the painful places and feeling the hard feelings were far from my natural instinct. But the bravest actions we take—the ones where we don't numb or avoid or deny but move fully into rawness and honesty—slowly help ease the pain. These courageous and horribly vulnerable moments actually purge the pain one tiny release at a time.

Not too long after Ben passed, I met his uncle Tom and aunt Debbie to go clean out his office at work. I knew it wouldn't be easy, but I'd also only been to Ben's office a few times to meet him for lunch or happy hour or a work Christmas party. It wasn't a hugely familiar place to me, so I thought maybe I'd be okay. Plus, I thought, I might as well get one of these awful must-dos over with.

As we came up to his office door, it was closed. The funeral program and a rustic-looking wreath hung on the front. I tried to reach for the door handle, but it was as if my mind and body had lost connection. For a minute I just stared, breathing deeply to fight back the tears. What I'd tried to convince myself wouldn't be a huge deal now felt completely overwhelming, another move toward a lifetime of painful, wobbly steps. I couldn't believe his colleagues actually wanted to see this as they passed by every day. Why hadn't they taken it down? Then, as if offering a gentle nudge, Tom, Debbie, and Ben's beloved boss, Deb, each hugged me and stood back. They graciously waited outside, allowing me the space to melt down in private before helping me pack up his things.

I opened the door and stepped into what felt like a perfectly preserved snapshot of the man I loved. One of simplicity and scattered snacks and endearing messiness—not because he wasn't organized but because often he was so excited to get on to the next

The joy does
come back. . . .
Eventually,
the pain isn't
the only voice
in the room.

———

thing that he didn't take time to tidy up the last. The walls weren't adorned with his law school credentials but were marked sparingly with some duck photos and a *Dead Poets Society* quote I had printed when he graduated law school.

"Medicine, law, business, engineering, these are noble pursuits and necessary to sustain life. But poetry, beauty, romance, love, these are what we stay alive for."[1]

Poetry aside, those last three were the essence of who Ben was and what he cared about—the beauty of nature, the romance of life and activity and adventure, and the simple yet sincere love he poured out on everyone he knew.

On his desk sat a few files, a photo of me from our wedding day, a duck-dog training book, and his Bible. Though he took great pride in his work, stepping into this frame of his day-to-day reinforced one of the great truths Ben taught me: the people we walk with enrich our lives much more than what we do or accomplish. People first, performance second. He knew this. He *lived* this.

As I slumped down in his desk chair, weeping and wondering how to pull it together with the others waiting outside, I uttered the one thing I wished I could tell him: "I'm so proud of you." Words he told me daily, and words I longed for him to hear me say one more time.

In that moment, in voicing how devastated I was yet how honored I felt to call him my husband, it was as if the suffocating cloud of sadness bearing down on me in that room lifted. In my whisper of gratitude for who God made Ben to be in the place where he lived it out each day, I found a little relief. I'd endured a painful step, and to my surprise, I found some strength on the other side.

These are the moments that, though painful and clumsy, start ushering us toward life, toward little sparks of joy. And the only way we can take them is one at a time. When we're grieving, sometimes the only thing we're able to do is shuffle. We can move slowly toward the reality that deep down we long to deny. We can keep stumbling in the right direction. It will always hurt, but it won't always hurt this much. We are on an arduous path of rehab, friends, and we won't make it if we're trying to run too fast.

Since then I've lived through thousands of tough steps and years of sloppy shuffling. And it was in moments like holidays with Ben's friends and cleaning out his office that I gradually began to feel again, not just function. These brave moments brought me back to consciousness. They made me feel real hurt but also real hope, sharp now but no longer surreal.

As the Lord began to coax me forward and mend my amputation, it began to feel a little less like a raw gash and a little more like scar tissue. I can now tell my story and watch *Yellowstone* and be with his friends, and I'm okay.

As much as I long for explanation, the Lord has not apologized or justified the amputation, but he has begun to teach me how to walk again. It's not a pretty walk. I won't be running any marathons. But with time I've learned how to move with full feeling and less fear, and I know now that each brave step brings with it a little more joy alongside the pain.

four

GOD NODS AND TREE STANDS

WHERE IS GOD?

As for me, I would seek God,
and to God would I commit my cause,
who does great things and unsearchable,
marvelous things without number.

JOB 5:8–9

When fundamental parts of our lives are lost, when people and things we thought we'd never lose are suddenly gone, it's natural to want answers. *Why did this happen? Who's to blame? What could I have done differently?* And for many of us in the aftermath of traumatic change, we also want to know, *Where is God? Where was he when the tragedy happened, and where is he now in my darkest days of hurt, when I'm longing for comfort?* When I am on

49

the floor, writhing in tears with no idea what the rest of my life will look like, where is God?

Wherever we are in our faith—secure, skeptical, or somewhere in between—suffering has a way of pulling us out of our comfort zones with God and forcing us to face how real and how reliable we believe he is in our day-to-day lives. Is he still here? Even with three decades of faith under my belt, grappling with this question hasn't always been easy. In my mind I know God is good and that he promises always, in every moment, to be with me. But when my vision seemed clouded with pain and questions, my eyes had a hard time seeing what my mind said was true.

When I did go looking for God, he was in some expected places—Scripture, prayer, listening to songs of worship. But even these regular spiritual rhythms that had been routine for much of my life proved a struggle sometimes. Seeking God and his presence isn't passive. It usually requires participation. He will open the door, but we have to knock. He is ready and willing to meet us exactly where we are, but I was in a weary and fragile place. Even when you have a strong desire to find God and feel God, grief is a complete attack on your mental and physical faculties. It left me with no energy or focus. I felt depleted in so many ways that my time with the Lord often felt desperate at best and forced at worse. But as we've learned, when we show up, he shows up too.

If you're honest with yourself, you may not feel ready to go to Scripture. You may not be ready to sing or pray or do anything active to pursue God. You may still be so hurt by God or distrusting of him that you're wary to step into spiritual places. But let me assure you: there is still hope. He is still with you, and you can still find him in places far outside the spiritual box.

We are all wired with a desire to know and see God. He built us that way. And though we don't always acknowledge it, that desire is hugely heightened when we suffer. Like a young child hurt or afraid, we crave the comfort of our Parent's arms. We can deny it, rely on ourselves and our own strength, and turn from God. Or we can accept how desperately we need his comfort, ask him for what we need, and keep our eyes open to see his provision. This is how we will see that the God who loves us is still right here. His comfort is still ready and available for the taking.

At least that's what it took for me. Not long after Ben's death, I was gifted a memoir by a local pastor, Steve Berger, and his wife, Sarah, written after losing their nineteen-year-old son. Still mentally and emotionally drained, I committed to reading it only because it was thin, a quick read. In *Have Heart: Bridging the Gulf Between Heaven and Earth*, the Bergers share a funny but profound anecdote about a member of their church community who lost her husband to organ failure.

As the woman faced her husband's impending death, she asked just one thing of him (and, ultimately, of Jesus): "Can you please send me a sign to let me know you are all right?"[1] This woman knew well her husband's salvation story as a biker-gang felon turned committed Christ follower. She knew exactly where he was going once his body passed away. But in the face of her coming heartbreak and despair, she boldly named what she needed—divine assurance of her husband's arrival home.

Not long after the burial service, the newly widowed woman was greeted by two unexpected guests in the hallway of her urban Orange County residence. She was home with her daughters when one of the girls stumbled on something strange in the hallway: two baby possums. Apparently, the woman wasn't much of a dog or cat person but had always wanted to raise possums as pets. What may seem to us like a crazy coincidence was, in reality, just what this grieving woman needed to find a little peace amid her pain. In the Lord's intimate, mind-blowing way, he answered her desperate plea for assurance with possums, a bizarre confirmation that could only be attributed to the work of his hands.

This sealed it for me. After reading of the possums, my only prayer became, *Lord, just give me my possum.* Even though I knew without a shadow of a doubt that Ben had been saved, I longed for assurances that he was home—confidence that he was peaceful, perfect, and so overwhelmed with the joy of Jesus that he wouldn't come back here even if he had the option. Though I still struggled to find words to pray in those early days, I continued asking for a possum.

Through this possum quest, I started to understand that seeking God doesn't have to be reverent or hyperspiritual. Sometimes the most honest way to seek God is by coming to him bluntly and telling him exactly what your broken heart needs.

It turned out that my possums were turkeys. I had been asking God for weeks for some sort of physical confirmation that Ben was home, and one gloomy, fall afternoon, God answered my plea. The sky was grim and rainy; it was a day when birds would have hunkered down for shelter deep within the trees. As I backed out of our driveway not a mile from one of Nashville's busiest commercial shopping areas, there they were—a whole group of turkeys, strutting across our neighbor's front yard, completely displaced from their natural, wooded, rural habitat.

Outlandish as this may sound, especially to those who don't love the outdoors, these turkeys confirmed all I needed to know and feel in that moment. Ben was an avid turkey hunter. In fact, the first time we ever went hunting together, we were chasing down turkeys.

Ben adored every moment he spent with his family in nature, and he tried his best to make me love it too. Those ugly birds in the driveway next door were God's gentle hush to my worried heart and his intimate confirmation that Ben was now filled with all-consuming joy, a joy infinitely greater than any he'd felt hunting here on earth.

As the birds trotted away, something in my spirit prompted me: *Mattie, how many?* Squinting and straining to see through the rain, I counted seven turkeys. Seven, the numeric date of our wedding day. The holy number of completion. The number I needed to remind me: God is not only with me but also in perfect control. To this day, on my worst days and in my most wrecked hours, I remember the turkeys. I remember the eternal joy my beloved is currently experiencing and will forever experience with Christ. I remember God's faithfulness to hear my need and his tenderness in reminding me he's never left me.

This was just the beginning of what our family has come to call *God nods*—quick, intimate, divine glimpses of God's care for us and his presence in our pain. Little moments in which the Lord provides reassurance or joy or peace despite the rawness of grief. Some of them came through books or songs or scenes in nature and some through dreams, both mine and countless others'. Like the turkeys, the God nods may sound like naive, wishful thinking to some who haven't experienced them, but in seasons of desperation for signs of God's goodness, they sustained me.

Ask for the assurances and the signs you need from the Lord. Ask that he would open your eyes to see them, and when you do, hold fast to them! They are the kindest, most personal, fatherly reminders that God cherishes us and that he's much closer in our suffering than we think. Receive these nods with gratitude. Relish them with joy. Record them so on the days when he feels lifetimes away you can relive the truth that your Living Hope is right here.

I will shout from the rooftops what Pastor Berger said and what all possum seekers like me hope to experience: "These kinds of special, supernatural moments radically contribute to the healing process. They come spontaneously and when we least expect them. . . . Recognize [and record] when God shows up in the midst of your sorrow."[2]

Much of my hope in those early days came from God nods like these. They started showing up all over the place once I kept my eyes open for God's little encouragements. When you're brave enough to ask, God is big enough to show up.

"CATCH YOU ON THE FLIP SIDE"

I'm a firm believer that the Lord communicates with all his children in different ways. I have never heard from him audibly or through prophetic vision. I'm much more often prompted quietly in my spirit, from a verse or a quote or a silent moment in prayer. But for months I prayed for the Lord to let me see my Ben in a dream. Countless close friends and family members had experienced God-given dreams of Ben since his passing, and by gosh, I thought I deserved one too! That may sound extreme or entitled, like I felt God owed me something—and at times, maybe I did. But after the turkey experience, I was reminded of what James told us about bringing our desires to God: "You do not have, because you do not ask" (James 4:2).

When we struggle to sense God's presence or see his hand in the midst of hardship, it's often because we forget the authority we have as his children. Like any good father, he wants to give us comfort and confirmation that he loves us and is with us.

> Blessed be the God and Father of our Lord Jesus Christ, the Father of mercies and God of all comfort, who comforts us in all our affliction. (2 Corinthians 1:3–4)

And while we can't expect him to meet our requests in the exact ways we want him to, he is always faithful to give us himself. We may not get the expected outcome of what we ask, but we will always find the comfort of his presence in the process of asking and opening our eyes.

The Lord brought me much peace through these dreams about Ben, some my own and some from friends and family. Some were extensively detailed and some uncomplicated and brief. But each felt uniquely and masterfully crafted with details personal to the one dreaming, and all delivered the resounding message, *Ben is home and safe with the Lord.*

For example, my cousin Angie, who works in real estate and helped Ben and me purchase our first home, dreamed she was showing a majestic house to Ben. He claimed it was "perfect in every way" and that he couldn't wait to show me, though he made it clear to Angie the time to show me wasn't yet. He was happy to wait for me to arrive in this glorious home he'd already found.

Then there was the dream the Lord sent Caroline, one of my absolute dearest friends and the one through whom he and I met. Ben and Caroline grew up together and remained very close until his death. They even referred to each other as "cousins," though there was no blood relation. In the dream, she and Ben were on her back patio at the house where he had lived with her and her husband for a summer (in fact, the same summer Ben and I met on that patio). Caroline says Ben was dressed as he always was in the summertime—in shorts, boots, and a baseball cap—with one leg hiked up on a pool chair. He grinned at her with his silly, boyish smile and greeted her as usual: "Hey, cuz!"

To which she asked, taken aback, "Hey, Benny. Whatcha doin'?"

With another grin and nod of the head, he assured her, "I just wanted to tell you not to worry about me. I'm doing just fine." Before she could reply or press him further, he gave her a wink and a casual, "Catch you on the flip side!"—the same way they always said goodbye. It was a simple, playful yet personal assurance to her that he was home and she'd see him again.

Sam, one of Ben's best friends and now my sister's husband, also dreamed of Ben's visit from heaven. In the dream, Sam found himself frantically searching for me, my sisters, and my mom in a crowded hospital. Sam raced into the elevator, unsure why he felt so compelled to get there quickly. Over his shoulder he looked and saw a young man in a camouflage hat, one with a hunting emblem Sam recognized right away.

"Ben?" he asked, very unsettled. "Where have you been?"

"Man," Ben replied, "I've been in heaven for a few days. Just been checking it out, and it's awesome!"

The elevator door opened, and Ben walked out. "Wait!" Sam jumped out after him. "Where are you going?"

Without looking back, Ben shouted to him, "I'm going to find the girls, so they know I'm okay too."

Sam was the only non–family member who saw Ben during his days in the ICU. A few afternoons he sat beside him recalling stories of their adventures hunting and fishing together so I could go shower and eat. Of course, the Lord brought him and him alone confirmation of Ben's first few cheerful days in heaven, in a dream, in the hospital.

But one experience in particular, the greatest God nod, came through our dear friend Patrick. Patrick and Ben grew up together, lived together in college, and were groomsmen in each other's weddings. Below are the exact details Patrick recorded when he woke early the morning of October 7, the morning of what would have been mine and Ben's first anniversary.

The dream starts out with me [Patrick] and John Floyd [another groomsman] in a room together. There is some sort of event that's about to start, but I'm not sure what it is yet. I pull out my blue tuxedo that I wore at Ben and Mattie's wedding. It looks a little dusty, as if it has been sitting in a closet for some time. The right lapel is a little wrinkled and has a crease in it.

I look to John and say, "We haven't worn these in a while. Why don't we just wear them for this thing today?" For some reason it feels fitting that we should wear them. He's excited and thinks it's a great idea.

We come out of the room we are in and step into the lobby of what feels like a church but also like the entrance into some type of garden. It starts to feel like we are here for a wedding, but it seems different. It has a sort of funeral feel, too, but in a celebratory, remembrance kind of way.

John and I are lined up, just us two, like we are groomsmen about to walk down the aisle, wearing our blue tuxedoes. The doors then open and an old country song starts playing. I'm not sure what the song is, but there is clearly a steel guitar sticking out above the rest of the melody.

We start walking down the aisle. There are five or six rows

of folded-out white chairs, maybe ten people per row on each side. It still feels like we're in both a church and a garden. We are both smiling because the country music seems so fitting for the event.

At the end of the aisle is a small stage with two steps leading up to it. We come up the steps and stand on the left side of the stage if you're facing it. Then Ben appears beside us. I turn to him, and he looks so excited and happy. He turns to me and gives me one of his really strong hugs and a kiss on the cheek. He is also wearing his blue tuxedo, and I realize we are definitely here for a wedding.

We stand facing the guests as if we are waiting for Mattie to walk down the aisle. Then I look to my left and onstage next to Ben, also on his left, is a beautiful flower arrangement. I wonder why it's placed there because it's right where I thought Mattie was supposed to stand.

Then I see someone standing on the other side of the flowers. I can't fully make out who it is because the arrangement is so big and beautiful. The person is sitting in a chair, and at first look, it appears to be a woman with golden hair wearing beautiful white and golden robes. I am awestruck at the beauty. I still can't fully see who it is with the flowers blocking my view, but whoever it is is beautiful and has a profound peace about them.

I look back at Ben, and he is smiling so big back at me. He says, "I love you, brother," just like he always did. My eyes are then opened, and I realize the person on the other side of the flowers is Jesus, the Bridegroom. At that moment both Ben and Jesus disappear, leaving together. I knew then why we were there that day. Everything felt so peaceful and right.

To echo Patrick's wife, Anne Walker, "Patrick literally doesn't dream. And if he does, he never remembers them." To say this divine, Scripture-resounding vision was a God nod feels like a massive understatement. I and so many others since have clung to this picture of Ben's ascension and unification with Jesus, our ultimate Groom, just as Revelation 21 promises will happen for all believers in the new heaven and new earth.

You may wonder how I knew these nods and dreams were from God. They may sound more like wishful thinking or like nice stories we told ourselves to soften the hurt. The truth is, I can't prove to you they were God nods, but I can assure you that the physical peace that came through these experiences, both to me and to others, was more than enough for me to accept they were gifts from the Lord. With them came a literal sense of stillness and relief that I know can only come from the Holy Spirit. No story we tell ourselves can calm the chaos of suffering. If you experience these things and, in turn, feel peace and assurance that you can't explain, I urge you not to question. Thank your ever-present, good Father for them, and rest.

Experiencing God in suffering will not look the same for everyone. Some may have clear confirmations from the Lord, like the God nods, and some may struggle for long seasons where he feels silent. I'm not suggesting a magic formula to hear from God or get what you want from him; rather, I'm offering my honest experience of how I learned to ask for the comfort I needed from my heavenly Father and trust he was able to provide it. I share these stories simply to say: never fear asking for the assurances your grieving heart needs. The promises of God are true, and it overjoys our Father to confirm that truth to you in intimate ways. He wants us to rejoice, even as we mourn. He wants us to taste and see his goodness (Psalm 34:8), even as we drink our bitter cup. Ask him to reveal himself to you, bold in faith that he will do it in his way, in his timing.

WATCHING THE WORLD WAKE UP

What about when the God nods seem to stop? Or worse yet, what if you get silence? Are you back at square one, waiting and wondering where God is in your suffering? Not everyone experiences the Lord the same way, and the Lord does not answer everyone's prayers in the same way. So if you find yourself struggling to pray or ask for what you need, or if you've been asking and no answer seems to come, I encourage you to shift your eyes from God the Comforter to God the Creator.

Sometimes our pain is so loud and our lack of understanding so consuming that we struggle to accept God as a comforting Father. We know all he does is for our ultimate good (Romans 8:28), but we can't help but feel betrayed by the one who could have protected us. As it did me, it may take you a while to work back into the rhythms of prayer and really trust the God on the other end. And that's okay. Even if you're still hurt and feeling resistant to communication with the Lord, I assure you, he is still with you, and there is still a place you can find him. You only need to step outside.

Nature has been integral in my healing process, partially because the outdoors was a big part of our marriage but also because creation is the primary physical way that humans experience God. The first things we learn about God in Scripture are through the story of creation in Genesis 1 and 2. We witness his power, his wisdom, and his intimacy and intentionality with all he creates.

Never fear
asking for the
assurances
your grieving
heart needs.

———

And just as we see his fingerprints in Genesis, so we can still see his power, wisdom, intimacy, and intentionality in the world around us. Something about seeing the gentle care with which God keeps creation has proved such a sweet reminder of how gentle and careful he is with me, even when it doesn't feel like it.

Grand mountain ranges and powerful ocean waves—how strong is God to carry us through our suffering? Sunrises and sunsets—how faithful is God to always show up in our time of need? Waterfalls and cool mountain springs—how generous is our God to continually fill us up when we feel empty? But don't think for a minute seeking God in the world around us demands extravagant vacations or glamorous landscapes. The God who knows every hair on our heads (Luke 12:7) is just as much in the mundane as he is the majestic.

This was something Ben always knew. "Isn't it amazing?" Ben said the first time he dragged me along hunting with him. "We're watching the world wake up!" Though his enthusiasm was endearing, we could not have held more different perspectives on the situation.

We weren't married yet—obviously, since I agreed to go hunting. (Once you're married, you get a get-out-of-hunting-free card.) It was April, and the morning proved dark, dewy, and far colder than I would have preferred. We barricaded ourselves beneath branches, Ben right at the tree line and me nestled among gnarled roots and wet leaves just at his back. Once you're in position, the game goes something like this: freeze, wait, continue to reposition rocks and sticks puncturing your lower back, wait more, hike in silence to find a better spot, hunker down among more trees, shoot ugly turkeys.

Needless to say, somewhere amid the cold, wet waiting, I missed the magical moment when the world woke up. But despite my discomfort, I knew the pure contentment Ben found out in the woods. It was a place of solitude and reverence for him. A place where he was physically part of God's handiwork. Later, that place would bring me unexpected peace when, just weeks after Ben died, I found the Lord in a tree stand.

Trust me, this shocked me as much as it may shock you. Though I'm a bit more seasoned now, I was never a hunter or camper or anything of the sort before meeting Ben. I only went hunting with him twice—the first time, when we shot our "double" turkeys, and the second on our honeymoon. My third experience came two months after he passed. It was the week of Thanksgiving, and I was defeated. I'd expected each "first" to feel worse without him, but the week leading up to that first holiday, I was hollow. There was nothing inside me but empty, unfillable, primal hurt. My head had plenty of things to be thankful for. My heart had none. I cried more that week than I had since I'd told him goodbye.

But the morning before Thanksgiving, I got a text from my sister's now-husband, Sam: "Deer hunt in the AM?"

My immediate reply? "Finding warm camo."

When you love someone, their world becomes yours in more ways than you anticipate. The family, the finances, the stuff—all of that is expected. But with time, your separate interests beautifully reshape into a whole new being, with whole new shared perspectives and enjoyment. So that morning, I opened up Ben's hunting closet for the first time since he'd passed. I clutched his clothes tightly to my face, inhaling and longing for a familiar scent. Some pieces I recognized as Christmas or birthday gifts from recent years. Some I thought he must've had since high school. A few pullovers, camo bibs, and one huge SITKA coat later, I was ready. I had no intention of finding God in the woods that day, but maybe I could find a little bit of Ben out there.

The morning of our hunt was the first below-freezing day of the season, a bone-chilling cold that made me consider turning right back to the house. But with Sam's help, I climbed up, strapped myself into Ben's stand, and began to wait. All I could think about was how much he loved this place, loved the woods, and would have loved to share this part of his life with me. I wanted him there with me now. I wanted him to know I would have gone with him more while he was here, had I known.

After what felt like hours of no warmth and no deer, my sadness grew to frustration. At that point I was only in it for the kill. I was going to bring home one final trophy to prove that I could do this on my own, that I could make Ben proud, that I was strong. But as my frustration began to build, a precious ray of sunlight pierced the murky fog, and I remembered: I wasn't there to prove myself; I was there to watch the world wake up. And as the warmth slowly came and the sun-kissed leaves glistened, I realized I wasn't just there to find Ben. I was there for the Lord to find me. I was there to be reminded that even in our coldest and most fruitless seasons, he is always there to bring light and warmth. He is waiting in the nuances of creation to meet us wherever we are. Ben knew that. He loved that about the outdoors. And from that day forward, I've loved it too.

There is such comfort to be found in the folds of God's creation. There is proof of his strength and faithfulness and promise to provide us what we need. That day in a tree stand, fifteen feet above cold, wet ground, I felt a joy that transcended time and loss. The outing wasn't about proving my strength but about letting the Lord, in his slow and sometimes painful way, wake up a part of me I didn't know had drifted to sleep, a part of me that had forgotten where to find him. And since that day, the trees, the flowers, the masterfully painted skylines continue to remind me that God, the Creator and the Comforter, is always around. Even when I don't hear him or get obvious God nods, he is only a quick prayer or an afternoon walk away.

It's easy to feel abandoned by God or think he has shrunk back from the messiness of your suffering. It's easy to feel distant from or resistant to him in the wake of what you've lost. But never for a minute believe the lie that he's left you. He is right beside you, ready and waiting for you to ask him for what you need and to meet you with light and warmth right in the middle of his glorious creation.

five

CLUTCHING PAPER ROSES

DOES TIME REALLY HEAL?

And after you have suffered a little
while, the God of all grace, who has
called you to his eternal glory in
Christ, will himself restore, confirm,
strengthen, and establish you.

1 PETER 5:10

We all have a chronic case of "Are we there yet?" When will I finally get that big promotion? How long will I have to stay single? How long will my heart feel broken? How long, how long, how long? It's our resounding cry as mortal beings. We hate waiting, and we long to know when we'll get from A to B, start to finish, hurt to healing. We are this way now, and we've been this way since Jesus' time.

Even as the all-knowing Messiah, Jesus didn't give his followers specific timetables. In the face of his impending death, he casually clued in the disciples that he would be back "in a little while." The Savior of all humanity, the only man to ever walk with men and be of God, offered no assurance of a specific time for his return. All he offered his closest eleven friends was, "In a little while you will see me no more, and then after a little while you will see me" (John 16:16 NIV). Gee, thanks for the foolproof direction there, Jesus. Not surprisingly, his followers went on to question what he meant, why he said it, and how long they'd have to wait to see him again.

Jesus didn't give the disciples a schedule or a road map for the hardship they were about to face. They would soon lose the man they'd committed their lives to follow, and they had no idea how long they'd have to wait for his return. Does this feel as stressful for us as it did for the disciples? Absolutely. We want to know how long we'll weep, how long we'll hurt, how long our lives will feel upended and full of sour lemons. But suffering is never scheduled, and pain is often healed at a much slower pace than we'd prefer.

We've all heard and likely subscribed to the idea that time heals all wounds. But is it true? Are we really left at the mercy of another month, another year passing before we'll begin to feel stable and like ourselves again?

Early on in my grief, I hated this idea. In fact, I flat-out rejected it. I didn't trust time to heal me because I wanted desperately to feel okay again, and soon. I wanted to flip a switch so that the endless triggers would stop. So that I could listen to country music again or eat Jet's Pizza again or go to church again without losing it. I wanted instant relief from all the things that reminded me of Ben and left me living on eggshells, constantly waiting for the next sting of sadness to hit.

And while grief is messy and healing is in no way instant, for me, time did begin to soften the edges of my pain, which for so long felt fatally sharp. Eventually I did find more still moments, more instances and hours and days with tastes of normalcy, even happiness. But these moments didn't come quickly, and they were rarely a result of my own efforts.

As time moved forward, I had no choice but to face my painful new reality head-on. The more I embraced each hurt—big and small—the more time taught me how to handle it. What to expect. How to grieve well and how to nurse my heart back to health. Time didn't take the pain away so much as it made the pain more manageable.

Time is crucial to our healing, both in understanding our hurt and in learning how we must personally process our grief. Nothing revealed that to me more clearly than going through the firsts. We are a culture of firsts after all: new life, new job, new love. Yet in the wake of loss, we grievingly turn from celebrating what is to mourning what isn't.

"The first year will be the worst," people said. "The holidays will feel the hardest." Was this a warning for the days just ahead or a glimmer of hope for all the holidays years down the road? Did this mean time really would heal my broken heart but it would hurt before it helped? Was it actually true?

Yes to all of the above.

The firsts were the hardest. Not because the pain was any worse on these days but because days that had previously been defined by celebration suddenly felt void of it. Days that should have marked the completion of another year of life instead magnified the life that had been cut off. Within the first three months after Ben passed, I faced our first anniversary, Thanksgiving, and Christmas. There was absolutely no way around it—they were all brutal, like surgery without anesthesia. Not that this should have come as any surprise. Everyone had warned me, right? They'd prayed, texted, sent cards that wished "get well" but whispered "get ready."

It turned out that the days leading up to the firsts were nearly as bad as the firsts themselves. As with any trial or painful thing we know is coming, the anticipation of impact sometimes hurts worse than the actual impact. Putting up decorations, parties with family and friends, shopping for and wrapping up gifts—none of which had Ben's name on them—these regular holiday rhythms left me overwhelmed with anxiety as the actual days of celebration approached. The anticipation of how bad it would be, how depressed I would feel, seized my every thought. So I dug in my heels and filled up my calendar, hoping that maybe time would hold off and I wouldn't have to do these days without him. I dreaded facing them and hated the fact that these holidays might never feel entirely full for me again.

Then the day itself would arrive. Breakfast would be made, coffee poured, and family would begin to gather. Truth be told, I felt empty. But in God's grace and in ways I don't understand, he still met me on those days, and through the love of those around me, he began to fill me back up. The warmth of all of those still with me helped me endure these firsts as people made kind, awkward efforts to include Ben in conversation. They were adapting to the "new normal," not pretending that these celebrations were at all like years past. There was restored and reworked compassion among everyone who loved him that ushered in little moments of peace, even as we hurt and mourned and cried.

But I had to lead the pack. I had to talk about Ben, smile about him, include him in blessings and laughter and stories. If there is true tenderness among you, and I pray there is, your friends and family will follow your lead and give efforts to foster some joy with the sorrow, whatever that looks like for you.

I survived those days, as messy as they looked. I had gotten through, so I thought that surely there must be some relief to come. *That must be the worst,* I told myself. *Thank God I've come out on the other side.* But as the decor came down and relatives left and friends went back to work, the letdown set in. It was an emotional hangover of epic proportions. I'd gone from empty to full to empty again. I had survived an intimate season without him, and in doing so, acknowledged what I'd denied since the day he died: the verdict of a life without him was final. Until Ben and I meet again, I will miss him every year on these days, as well as so many others.

But in surviving those firsts, as sad and depleted as they left me, I felt more confident that I could face these days again. The holidays and their emotional aftermath slowly built back strength in me, little by little, day by day. I started to understand that to survive these firsts was not just to stagger through, avoiding fatal injury; rather, straining and exhausting my heart on these days broke it down and restored it to a sturdier foundation.

I trust fully the Lord's ability to take my fragile heart and bolster it in ways only he can. Many days I feel anything but strong, anything but sturdy. But I survived the firsts, and I have full faith that the Lord will continue to carry me through the hard days and build back my muscles even stronger with each season that passes.

Back then, I hoped desperately this was true—and now I know it is. Our first wedding anniversary—October 7, 2018— was just three weeks after Ben died. Only a year before, I'd felt

I trust fully the
Lord's ability
to take my
fragile heart and
bolster it in ways
only he can.

———

more joy, more wholeness, more anticipation for the future than I knew possible. But this day was bleak, empty, and entirely full of uncertainty.

This is one of the details that takes people's breath away when I share my story. Not only had I lost at twenty-eight what most enjoy for decades, I had a mere three weeks before having to "celebrate" the happiest day of my life, alone, devastated, and completely lost.

But celebrate I did. If time wasn't going to stop on my behalf, I knew the pain wasn't going to either. It was going to be agonizing no matter what I did, so I'd be damned if I was going to let it only hurt. I could at least do my part to find a smile somewhere in the day.

I'd planned a dinner with girlfriends and family for that evening, my best attempt to turn gut-wrenching reality into a reason to remember. We ate and laughed and poured beautiful South African wines that Ben and I had brought home from our honeymoon. But earlier that day, when the sun had come up and the only person I wanted to celebrate with wasn't there, I knew I wasn't ready for a dinner party. Nothing in me felt like celebrating. I needed to face the ugliest parts of my pain and let them out if I'd have any hope to enjoy a single moment of the night's plans.

So I watched our wedding video. The whole hour-and-a-half-long, magnificent, painful thing. I sat in our basement at nine in the morning, clutching the sweet bouquet of paper roses made from hymnal pages that Ben had ordered for our "paper anniversary" nearly two months before. (If you're married you know this is a miracle in and of itself, as most men do not plan gifts two months in advance.) When the box from Etsy had arrived earlier in the summer, I'd wondered, *What on earth did he order from Etsy?* Ben sternly warned me not to open it, and I'd actually forgotten about it until arriving home from the hospital after he passed. I didn't open it until the morning of our anniversary, and I have never felt rawer yet more loved and seen than I did when I pulled out that bouquet. Loved and seen by Ben. Loved and seen by God. Both of them, in different ways of course, knew I needed to hold that physical emblem of our marriage. The Lord knew it would serve as Ben's last, intimate gift to me, and Ben simply knew it would make me smile. It still sits on my desk beside his picture as one of my absolute greatest treasures.

As I watched the video, I held the flowers and sipped champagne and sobbed uncontrollably. I saw him smile and giggle at our first look and watched him wipe away tears as I walked down the aisle and into his arms. I watched us exchange rings and say our vows under a grand arch of white roses. I heard him pray for our marriage and our lives as we quietly took Communion. I saw him dance and sing and burst into rooms in the grand way that I will always miss.

Watching the video that day was the hardest thing I've done since he died. Harder than sitting through the funeral and burial. Harder than leaving our home and packing his things. Harder than learning to use the word "I" instead of "we," "mine" instead of "ours."

The anniversaries since have looked the same in many ways but different in others. I still watch our video and hold the paper roses. I'm still sure to meet my sorrows in the morning, open and raw, just myself and the Lord. I still plan lunches and dinners and afternoon walks with people I love, people who loved Ben too. And with each of the passing years, I've learned how to hold the hurt and remember that time is on my side. I've learned that as October 7 comes again and again and again, I will make it. The Lord is with me, my people are with me, and each year, I'll be a little bit stronger and smile a little bit more than the last.

A LIFETIME OF PAPER CUTS

Like the anniversaries and all the other firsts, the everyday pains that strike out of nowhere have also lessened with time. But for a while, these "small things" were huge. They were like paper cuts, personal reminders that most couldn't see but that cut me just as deeply as the firsts. They came on in an instant, feeling uncontrollable and endless for many, many months. I've since lived with years' worth of emotional assaults, each coming on quickly but their sting hanging around.

Were the firsts really the hardest? To a degree, yes; to the same degree that being hit in the arm with a baseball bat hurts worse than a thousand paper cuts.

You see, the important things—the holidays and the firsts—*were* devastating, direct hits, debilitating on impact. They stopped time and arrested my vision, zeroing in on all that I'd lost. The special days weren't worse than the daily triggers; they were simply expected. I knew they were coming, braced myself, and tried as best I could to "prepare" for the blow.

But the paper cuts gave no warning. No time to ready myself or pep-talk my heart. They were instant and intimate, an unending ambush. To others they may have seemed to be surface-level cuts, that is if others could see the wounds at all. Through no fault of their own, what their eyes assessed as a scratch felt to me like a gaping incision. For so long my daily rhythms were marked by unanticipated attacks—subtle, stinging reminders that Ben was gone.

Taking out the trash, checking the mail, picking up the dog at the vet. Mowing the grass or scraping off the grill. All the things Ben did that had then seemed forgettable now felt so significant. Each one reinforced my being alone.

Crying and changing an outfit last minute because I couldn't zip my dress or hook my bracelet. Taking three trips up and down the stairs to load and unload the car from a trip. Trying to bathe a rambunctious dog. Things that used to be easy with four hands now felt impossible with two.

And it wasn't just the tasks, the things Ben did, but also the things he loved—songs, meals, movies—that reminded me of his absence. I even burst into tears at the grocery when passing the little Halos oranges I used to buy him to snack on at work. I completely lost it getting a back massage at a reflexology spa because the masseuse popped my fingers in the same way Ben used to pop them. I quickly realized while listening to girlfriends talk about sex with their husbands that what I physically missed more than anything was a real hug—a hug from the one who knew me so sensually but just wanted to hold me in his arms.

These daily triggers are endless, and they cut deeper than I ever anticipated. But like the firsts, the paper cuts, too, bring healing with time—new rhythms and routines; muscles rebuilt that I didn't know had atrophied, that outsiders can't see; a whole list of things that I couldn't do until I had to. And I celebrate them! I no longer chalk them up as insignificant or trivial. I cut a piece of cake and thank the Lord because I have persevered in one more small way. This, I believe, will be how I heal: not just by surviving the anniversaries but by facing and embracing one paper cut at a time with tears and resilience and honesty. By acknowledging how deep those little cuts are and having faith that as I endure them, they will eventually scab over.

As much as I wish there were, there is no big revelation or fix-it moment in grief. No one instant of turning a page from hurt to healed. But there is time. And as we clutch paper roses and endure the paper cuts, with faith and confidence that we will survive them, the Lord builds back our resilience and our capacity for joy. Time will never take our pain away, but it teaches us how to handle the pain, how to endure and hurt well. I have experienced how powerfully time can contribute to healing, and if we face the pain fully and vulnerably, we will one day look up and be stronger than we thought we'd ever be again.

six

A BETTER NAME

WHO AM I NOW?

To them I will give in My house and within My walls a memorial,
And a name better than that of sons and daughters;
I will give them an everlasting name which will not be eliminated.

ISAIAH 56:5 NASB

For the first several months without Ben, I was learning what to do. Through the firsts and the paper cuts, I was learning how to hurt, how to grieve, how to process living without the person I loved. I was learning to both show up and to rest. I was learning how to let people into my pain and not worry whether they could handle it or not. I was learning to ask God for exactly what I needed and to open my eyes to see his faithfulness and assurance and comfort. I was learning that time was on my side, and though the path to restoration would be slow, I was at least on my way.

I'd learned so much about suffering and faith and the constant fight of living in a broken world. I'd lost huge parts of my life that I would never get back. What I hadn't yet faced was how much of myself I'd also lost in the cross fire. I was gaining some footing on what to do but felt completely undone about who I was. My husband, my marriage, my future—I'd addressed losing those things as best I knew how, but what about all the parts of my identity I lost with them? It was as if all of a sudden the main labels on my life were ripped off, and I was left with a white sticker, a Sharpie, and no idea what to write in the blank. I was still the same Mattie, of course, but I felt so utterly different.

I never expected, in the wake of all the other changes, that how I saw myself would change too. I didn't realize until I asked the hard question—*Who am I now?*—how much value I had assigned to my labels. The labels of *wife* and *caretaker*—and down the road, *mother*—that I'd clung to so tightly. I began to see I had invested much of my identity in what I did and the person I did things for. And now that person and those responsibilities were gone.

Not only did I long for the labels I'd lost, I hated the one I had gained: *widow.*

It took months for me say the word out loud. I hated the sound of it. I hated the uncomfortable, pitying look it brought to people's faces when they heard it. I hated that it made me feel like a victim of something that would never change. It felt unerasable. Too huge to hide and too permanent to ignore. I got used to dancing around the word with "my husband passed away" or "I lost my husband X amount of time ago." I wanted desperately for *widow* not to be part of who I was and how people saw me.

What's utterly painful though completely divine is that when I cofounded NaSHEville, a philanthropic women's apparel company, we felt led to financially give back to three specific groups through the sale of our merchandise: orphans, victims of human trafficking, and widows. We established these missions two months before Ben's accident. The call to serve widows wasn't something either Brooke (my business partner) or I had planned, but when we went to Scripture, we saw over and over God's call to take care of orphans and widows.

> Learn to do good;
> seek justice,
> > correct oppression;
> bring justice to the fatherless,
> > plead the widow's cause. (Isaiah 1:17)

Religion that is pure and undefiled before God the Father is this: to visit orphans and widows in their affliction. (James 1:27)

Clearly, this wasn't a coincidence. Before anything had happened to Ben, the Lord had placed me in a position to walk out widowhood in real time, in front of all our supporters, followers, and community. He gave me a platform and a voice to speak of real hurt, real struggle, and real hope before women of all ages who'd lost their spouses, and I did, to the best of my brokenhearted ability. But I still hated the word and avoided it at all costs. It was one thing to encourage others and meet them in the midst of their stories. That was safe because I was doing something. I was helping them and, in turn, finding some purpose from my pain. It was a whole other thing to call myself a widow. That was *being* something—something I wanted more than anything not to be. That meant widowhood was a part of who I was, not just a way to help others.

So, it really shouldn't have been a surprise when I heard it as my identifier only a few months after Ben died. Brooke and I were having coffee with some ladies who worked for a nonprofit our company partners with. I'll never forget that stomach-dropping, mouth-drying, face-flushing feeling of hearing, "Mattie is a widow too." My heart still beats heavily as I type these words. It's not that I wasn't inescapably aware it was true; it was just that hearing it out loud confirmed it was permanent. I felt in that moment—and every time I've uttered the word since—that it will never go away. *Will this always be who I am?*

I don't know if I will ever accept that label as a definitive part of me. I'm still working through it with the Lord, and I still want it to be untrue. I've felt embarrassed and afraid and frustrated about it for so long. But there was one moment in particular that brought me a little assurance. Maybe, eventually, I'd be seen as more than a young widow again.

It was the first time I'd gone back to church on my own. Going back at all was hard for me, even though I wanted to be there. I knew I needed to be there. But not only had we held Ben's funeral in my church's sanctuary, he and I had also joined as members there the summer before his accident. The place meant to usher us into new phases of life and set the stage for our family's faith community now made me feel all the more alone. Even with the church's overwhelming kindness and support, it was yet another place we'd sought out together that I now sat in without him.

It was months before I ever had to go alone. If I wasn't with friends, my family always ensured I had someone at my side on

Sundays. But even with them the sorrow and the strangeness of it was often unbearable. So many tears and so many tissues.

I knew continuing to bring a buddy to church wasn't realistic. One day I'd have to show up to worship as myself, not as a widow with a wingman. The first day I went alone, I didn't tell anyone else I was going. I snuck in late to the 8:30 a.m. service, which I didn't normally attend. I had my eyes set on one of the back rows but felt compelled to continue farther to the front. I found a spot at the end of a pew about halfway up, hoping I wouldn't have to scooch in to make room for more latecomers and be stuck between two big, happy families.

I've never been prone to anxiety, much less panic attacks, but this moment pressed in on me so physically that I could hardly breathe. My chest felt tight, my breath was short, and tears in my eyes immediately began to well. I felt so conspicuous and trapped, my heart pounding in a vacuum of loneliness. I tried to sing to jolt myself out of it, but the words of the sorrowful hymn just overwhelmed me more.

Just two more songs, I told myself. *Mouth the words and discreetly dab your eyes, and it will be over.*

Then as the last song began, I nearly jumped back at the sight of an older woman I'd never met coming across the aisle. She had been in the row directly to my right and must have seen my meltdown and felt sorry for me. She had thick, brown-rimmed glasses and a bright sweater that looked a lot like Tennessee Vols orange. Something about her felt safe.

"I know you don't know me, honey," she whispered, "but I know some of your good friends." It turned out that she had taught two of my best friends in high school—friends I had plans to see that very afternoon. We continued to make small talk, but the fact that she hadn't led with another "I'm sorry" or "I heard" was the permission I needed to finally exhale. The truth is she likely only knew my face because who forgets the twenty-eight-year-old widow? But that wasn't how she addressed me that morning. To her I was simply a friend of a friend—a label I have never been so relieved to put on.

She stayed with me for the rest of the service as if we'd known each other for years. Even when her husband came to join us, she simply introduced me as a friend—no label, no explanation, no pity.

I had been terrified to return to church alone. I physically panicked the moment I walked in. But in this brief interaction, I found a little bit of freedom from the new identity I wished I could throw away. Sure, being a widow will always be part of my story. It will always be part of who I am, but in one act of kindness from a stranger, the Lord reminded me it won't always be the biggest part of who I am. It won't always be the first thing people see or the one thing they remember about me. I could and would be just Mattie again; it just might take me a little while to find her.

BECOMING AUNT MATTIE

Not only did I feel labeled by what I'd lost, I also felt robbed of what I didn't get a chance to be. I am not a mother, but that, too, was part of my future with Ben that I had to let go of. Grieving something I never had was completely uncharted territory. We hadn't yet been trying for kids, but the family I'd forecasted and anticipated was his—and when your future finally has a face and a last name, you still feel like you've lost it even if you haven't had it yet.

Within moments of the surgeon telling us Ben was brain-dead,

I pled with God for a way to still have his child. One with his devoted heart, infectious smile, and generosity toward everyone around him. In a world where material success and excess and image dictate so much of our perceived worthiness, I longed for children wired with his sense of contentment. My family laughs now at how just about everything Ben did or ate or experienced was, in his words, "phenomenal." Nothing wasn't worth celebrating. The little things were big to him, and the everyday worth a toast.

Having Ben's child was my last hope to realize the family we'd planned for. To at least get to carry and hold and kiss one of the three kids whose names we'd already picked out. Maybe that would help me survive. I never actually asked the doctors to take his sperm. His body had already been through too much. But I did take three pregnancy tests in the weeks following, knowing all too well how unlikely a double line was but hoping desperately that maybe a miracle would come.

Once again, no miracle. All three tests were negative. How could I be so devastated by not having something that, a few weeks prior, I hadn't even felt ready for? Pregnancy was a last hope, a lifeline, and I was frantic for something, anything, to play out how I'd planned.

I never told anyone I took those tests. I think even then part of me knew having Ben's child without him would be more heart-breaking than comforting, but the plan we'd held off on pursuing hurt. Not only had I lost my chance at a family, but it seemed everywhere I turned, someone else was getting the chance to start theirs. Seven of my best friends had their first children in the first two years after Ben's death, and many of them have since had their second. I was thrilled for them, of course, but with every shower and every new baby, I was haunted by maternal longing. Every birth announcement made me feel as if I were watching others start to run a new, exciting race while I sat on the sideline.

I still struggle with this. Starting my life over while most around me build their families and live out this new, fulfilling part of their identities is brutal. But it's okay to lament missing out on what comes so naturally to those around us. It's good to grapple with who we are and be honest about the parts that hurt. As with every other struggle, if we bring it to the Lord and trust his goodness to heal in us what we can't heal for ourselves, he will meet our needs.

With lots of time and tears behind me, God continues to heal my desire and soften my pain with gentle reminders that a baby wouldn't fix me. How would I have raised him or her alone? What if the child couldn't fill the hole Ben left? What if missing out on the thing I desired most was, in fact, the most gracious hand the Lord could have dealt me?

Even in losing the chance to have children with Ben, the Lord has brought me another joy. He has put me in a new role. He has given me a new label that has helped me find contentment in who I am as I love on children who aren't my own. I may not be Mom, but I have found abundant joy and blessing in becoming Aunt Mattie to these kids. I join them for playdates and shower them with gifts. I receive finger paintings and homemade valentines and tape them up, covering every inch of my fridge. I watch them while their moms work or run errands. Simply by being in their lives, I've found rich glimpses and tastes of the life as a mom I still long for. Being Aunt Mattie doesn't take the sting of Ben's and my unrealized plans away. It doesn't change the fact that I still want my kids to have his eyes and laugh and last name. But the love I have for these families around me, and the way they intentionally include me in their lives, has made me feel like I belong somewhere again. It's reminded me that family is found anywhere doors and hearts stay open.

Accepting the loss of my future family has been a long and difficult journey—one that remains unfinished. I've logged years of prayer and ask the Lord daily to heal the wound of losing the chance for the children I wanted. It is a huge act of faith to surrender our identities and unanswered prayers to him. Doing so feels scary, uncertain, and reluctantly humbling. But it will bring healing, dear friends. Bring your losses and scars and stolen dreams to the Lord, and he will show up to soothe and repair the deepest wounds of your soul.

A NAME BETTER THAN ALL THE REST

Still today I struggle with the tendency to see myself as the labels I have or don't have. Every day takes effort accepting the word *widow* and maintaining hope that I can be a wife again and a mother down the road. In retrospect losing Ben revealed that I had invested too much in these roles—not that they are unimportant, but they were never intended to become my whole identity. And though I've done a lot of spiritual reorganizing in how I see and value myself, for a long time, I was still unsure about who I was, much less who I'd be moving forward. I felt a total reset button on my life had been pushed, and everything before me was a series of cruel question marks.

How do I learn to be single again? What if the me going forward looks different than the me I knew before? Do I still call myself Ben's wife? I hate the term late husband. *Do I use the prefix Mrs., or do I use Ms. now, as if I'm some dignified retiree? Do I continue to wear my wedding band, though legally I could remarry? Who am I going to be now?*

One morning as I was sitting with God, somewhat praying but mostly complaining, I broke down and asked a big question I could no longer hold back: *I've waited my whole life to reach this point, secure this role, and play out this part as a godly wife for the glory of your kingdom, Lord, and you just took that away. We were going to use our marriage to serve you! Why wouldn't you want that?*

And that's true. From the day we started dating, Ben and I would pray together each morning. Whether for five minutes or thirty seconds, at 5:00 a.m. long distance or 10:00 a.m. on a Saturday, we truly did build our relationship on God's Word. "Let us trust in the Lord with all our hearts and lean not on our own understanding. Help us make disciples of all nations. And thank you for friends and family we get to spend eternity with." That was Ben's daily prayer for us.

Now don't get me wrong—this paints a much holier picture of us than the rest of the twenty-three hours and fifty-something minutes of the day would show. But regardless of our struggles, flaws, failures, and straight-up sinful patterns, we longed to be the gospel picture of what God intended marriage to be. We weren't anywhere close to having achieved it, but we were striving for it, and God still let it be taken away.

So, I questioned him. *Anything but my marriage, Lord! Why take this?* I knew all the stories in the Bible where "the LORD gave, and the LORD has taken away" (Job 1:21), but I couldn't accept that I'd been added to the roster of those who had experienced the second part of that statement. I thought of Joseph, who, though faithful to God and loyal to his family, was sold into slavery by his own brothers and later falsely imprisoned by his Egyptian master,

Potiphar (Genesis 37, 39). Or Ruth, who selflessly left her home-land to care for her widowed mother-in-law in Bethlehem. Not only was she an outsider, a girl from Moab living in Judah, but she herself was a young widow, making her financially and physically vulnerable (Ruth 1). I knew these people were faithful, yet each lost foundational parts of their lives and identities and had to learn how to live again after their lives were painfully reset. Who was Joseph without his family and his freedom? Who was Ruth without her husband, home, and resources? Who was I supposed to be without my marriage?

I knew one day, like them, all I'd lost would be redeemed, but was I supposed to just accept Ben's death and wait around until then? I wanted to talk to God about it, to be still and hear him assure and console me. But even more than quiet assurance, I wanted answers. And for the first time, I got truly angry.

Up until that point, I hadn't really felt mad about Ben's death. Disappointed, confused, heartbroken, helpless? Absolutely. But not angry. My lack of anger wasn't because I was valiant or had a super mature faith. It just felt like too much effort to get upset with God about something he wasn't going to undo. But that morning as I sipped my coffee and prepared for my weekly Bible study group, my whys began sounding more like WTFs. I'll never forget that moment, seething as I read the first chapter of Job. The man who was heralded as "blameless and upright, one who feared God and turned away from evil" lost everything (Job 1:1). Because Satan chalked Job's faithfulness up to his wealth, health, and happiness, God allowed Job's entire life to be stolen away—his possessions, his career, his health, and every one of his children. I burned with betrayal as I read how God gave Satan rein over Job's life. I knew the story already, but as I read the exchange between the Father and the Enemy that morning, all I could hear was them speaking my name.

Satan coming to God to take from me. God gambling my faithfulness with the one who wants to steal, kill, and destroy me (John 10:10). I couldn't accept it. I wept. I yelled. I erupted. "What kind of Father are you that you'd let Satan come after me? Come after Ben? Come after my marriage? Am I a twenty-eight-year-old widow because I needed to prove my faith in some cruel test? Did you allow Satan to assault my life, or was Ben's fall really just an accident?"

And in the midst of my honest, raw, unfiltered frustration, the Holy Spirit countered my questioning with a question of his own: *Who are you?*

The Spirit prompted me again. But this time, *Whose are you? Whose am I?*

After a few minutes, my heavy breathing began to slow, and I felt the anger subside. God's answer to me was simple: *Mine. You are mine.* This wave of comfort rushed over me, feeling almost physical. The Lord was assuring me that I was his above all else, and that no loss or death or disaster would ever change that. He was reminding me of the one label, the single identity marker, that can never be taken away: daughter of the King. Jesus' whole life, death, and resurrection ensure that I no longer have to question who I am or where my worth is found. Because he has saved me, I am defined above all else as a member of his eternal family.

Paul said it this way in the book of Romans: "The Spirit himself bears witness with our spirit that we are children of God, and if children, then heirs—heirs of God and fellow heirs with Christ, provided we suffer with him in order that we may also be glorified with him" (8:16–17).

And like this in Ephesians: "Even as he chose us in him before

I was the
Lord's above
all else, and no
loss or death
or disaster
would ever
change that.

_____

the foundation of the world, that we should be holy and blameless before him. In love he predestined us for adoption to himself as sons through Jesus Christ" (1:4–5).

My identity as God's chosen, redeemed, adopted child always has been and always will be the cornerstone of who I am. Ultimately, it is the only place my true value lies. In him I know who I am. In him my course could be steady and straight as long as I kept asking the right question.

The only identifier, the only label, the only answer the Lord needed me to hear was the truth that I was his. His daughter, his beloved, his child to comfort and give peace, provision, and promise, even if my identity and future felt utterly uncertain. I could rest in the name Jesus bought for me with his blood, even as I mourned the loss of other parts of my identity.

> To them I will give in My house and within My walls a
>   memorial,
> And a name better than that of sons and daughters;
> I will give them an everlasting name which will not be
>   eliminated. (Isaiah 56:5 NASB)

Who I am looks different than it did before Ben's death, but I'm learning to keep the label of *whose I am* above all the others. We are each first and foremost children of God, chosen, beloved, adopted, and given an everlasting name. Acknowledging this didn't change anything about what I lost or make working through my new widow label easy, but it did bring to my attention the truth that my identity in Christ is always greater than my identity as a wife or future mom or widow or anything else.

If you are to have any peace, any clarity navigating how you see yourself after your life reset button is pushed, you must remember you are his, for now and for eternity. The earthly roles you hold that contribute to your value and identity are nothing compared to your role as a son or daughter of God. It is a painful struggle to find ourselves again after our lives are turned upside down, but God's daily assurance of *you're mine* can and will redeem our losses and restore our hearts.

DESPERATE ROOTS AND PRUNING BRANCHES

WHY DOES GOD ALLOW SUFFERING?

Not only that, but we rejoice in our
sufferings, knowing that suffering produces
endurance, and endurance produces
character, and character produces hope.

ROMANS 5:3–4

For six years after college, I worked in the food and wine indus-try. I grew up loving food, cooking, and creating, but wine was far from a staple in my parents' pantry. Nonetheless I fell in love with it. The history, the science, the culture—it all fascinated me.

When I was twenty-three, I even spent fall working the harvest with a prestigious winery in Napa Valley. Glamorous, right? Wrong.

Don't mishear me—it was the experience of a lifetime. But what most people don't know about wine is that the beautiful product it becomes is in no way reflective of the grueling place from which it begins. Grape growing is agriculture. It's farming. Wine making requires long days, early hours, and labor-intensive, dirty work—not just for those making the wine but for the poor grapes themselves. Often, the more the grapes "suffer" during development, the more opulent the finished product turns out to be.

You see, in cultivating premium wine grapes, stress is everything. Science shows that the highest-quality fruit comes from the sites of greatest struggle—steep, hillside vineyard blocks whose soil holds less nutrients and water than other fertile, or "comfortable," sites. These sites put just enough stress on the vine to strain the fruit and, most often, yield grapes of physiological superiority and strength. The key ingredients?

1. Deep, sturdy roots that reach below the stripped topsoil into the life-giving earth below. A hungry and thirsty foundation that grasps desperately for sustenance when all around it is barren.
2. Pruning, or cutting back parts of the branches, in order to eliminate weak fruit and excessive foliage that can block necessary sunlight.

This has been my experience through grief: rocky soil, desperate roots, and painfully pruning branches.

This is also the picture of endurance that Jesus himself painted for us in John 15.

Every branch in me that does not bear fruit he takes away, and every branch that does bear fruit he prunes, that it may bear more fruit. . . . Abide in me, and I in you. As the branch cannot bear fruit by itself, unless it abides in the vine, neither can you, unless you abide in me. I am the vine; you are the branches. Whoever abides in me and I in him, he it is that bears much fruit, for apart from me you can do nothing. (vv. 2, 4–5)

In seasons of depletion and brokenness, endurance comes not through what the branches can do for themselves but through the solidly rooted vine to which the branches are grafted and careful branch pruning done by the vintner. I would never have chosen this story for my life had God asked my opinion. I would never choose it for you or for anyone else. But my prayer for all of us in our barren, rocky seasons is that we remember that we are not the Vine Keeper. That we can exchange the pressure to hold ourselves together for the invitation to fall apart in our Father's arms. That we can hold the lament of what has passed with the hope of what is promised; the pain of what's been pruned away for the fruit we're hopeful will come. And ultimately, that we remember the most crucial part of our healing won't be in the strength of our branches but in the strength and desperation of our roots.

BUILDING BABY ROOTS

It's hard to tell from the surface how sturdy roots are until a storm comes, until lightning strikes and winds howl and trunks that otherwise looked solid and secure start to bend. I know this because I grew up with pretty traditional, Christian-girl roots. Sunday school, prayers at dinner and before bedtime, even a church camp now and then, which, if we're honest, was more about the social than the spiritual. I spent kindergarten through twelfth grade—thirteen years—at a Christian school, where we donned T-shirts with Bible verses, had a full week of "spiritual emphasis" each year, and split the high school students into teams called "Alpha" and "Omega" (Revelation 22:13) for ongoing athletic and academic competitions. Sounds like I had some awfully solid roots, right? Not as solid you may think.

I am overwhelmingly grateful that my childhood was rich with traditions and practices of faith. I am nothing but thankful that my parents laid this foundation for me, and I would not be the woman I am today without them, my teachers, and my friends fostering in me a heart to love Jesus. But the baby roots that brought me to faith at twelve could never have withstood the storm that struck me at twenty-eight. Even though I grew up in Christian culture, it took experiencing real hardship for those weak, surface-level roots to reach deep and grow secure.

No matter how you were raised, how long you've been in the faith, or whether you're still grappling with what you believe, God is ready and able to strengthen your roots. Like he did with me, he might start working on them before hardship comes your way, or he might meet you right in the middle of a storm you never saw coming and start building your faith from there. We serve a God who isn't afraid to let us struggle or be stressed because he knows that's how we grow into the richest version of ourselves. He knows that as our roots grow, we not only gain spiritual strength but also get to know him, the Vinedresser, even more intimately.

I love how the apostle Peter put it: "In this you rejoice, though now for a little while, if necessary, you have been grieved by various trials, so that the tested genuineness of your faith—more precious than gold that perishes though it is tested by fire—may be found to result in praise and glory and honor at the revelation of Jesus Christ" (1 Peter 1:6–7).

Trials build deep roots. Trials test our faith. Trials strain us and refine us.

The first season of root building for me came in December 2010, long before Ben and I met. Mom and Dad called me and my two younger sisters up to Dad's office one afternoon. We expected nothing but a schedule briefing for our family's annual Christmas visits. I was twenty, and my sisters were both teenagers. I was always a strong, level-headed kid, but nothing could have prepared me for the news that Mom had been diagnosed with colon cancer.

She was healthy and fit, and never in my lifetime could I even remember her being sick with more than a cold. I wish I could say I was able to lean into faith in the midst of crippling fear of what might happen to her, but I wasn't. I shut down.

Completely jarred by how sudden and unfair my mom's illness was, I ran—back to college, away from the fear, and, for a little while, away from God. My roots were weak. But what eventually strengthened them and helped make my fragile faith sturdy was watching Mom through the whole process. She wasn't angry at the Lord—or if she was, she certainly kept that between her and him. I saw firsthand the woman I admired more than anyone else completely abiding and trusting in God in her toughest season of suffering and uncertainty.

Her roots were deep. Her struggle with sickness didn't diminish her faith; it made it even more solid and radiant for others around her to witness. I now see that watching how graciously she endured diagnosis, treatment, and ultimately full remission (Praise Jesus!)

was the first major way the Lord began to strengthen me—my roots, my trust, and my baby faith that needed to gain a little muscle. And though I never vocalized it or gave it much thought back then, I wonder now: Was he using this experience to prepare me for inevitable sicknesses and deaths I'd face later in life? Was this proof of why God allows his children to suffer—to help build their roots?

I believe so! I believe in a sovereign God who uses all things, even bad things, for the good of those who love him (Romans 8:28). Walking alongside Mom during her treatment and recovery steadied my faith in big ways, and it began to shift my self-reliance toward God-reliance. This was my first time considering what John 15 tells us. *Maybe the strength isn't in the branches but actually in the Vine?*

Suffering can prompt us to make this shift. And suffering can not only embolden our faith but also reveal a richer, more intimate understanding of who God is. Yes, through Mom's cancer, I began relying on Jesus the protector, the Vine who steadies and sustains me. But not until losing Ben did I truly get to know Jesus my personal friend, the one who wants to reveal every part of himself to me.

In all the ways my friends and family were there for me and supported me, Jesus was the only one who could fill the gaping hole of grief I faced. In so many moments, I actually felt his presence with me. I began to know him not just as the one who saved me but as one who wants to sit beside me. He so gently holds my pain, the Wonderful Counselor. He gives me his strength when mine isn't enough, the Mighty God. He reminds me that all wrongs will be made right, the Everlasting Father. He is a physical calm in the chaos, the Prince of Peace (Isaiah 9:6).

Not until
losing Ben did
I truly get to
know Jesus my
personal friend,
the one who
wants to reveal
every part of
himself to me.

____

Trust me when I say, knowing Jesus more intimately is worth the tears we cry and storms we endure here on earth. He is not a consolation for what you've lost; he *is* a greater companion than you can ever imagine. I have never felt more reliant on God and more rooted in him than I do today. I have never experienced Christ in such a personal, transformative way. Through my loss my roots have deepened. And yours can too if you rely on and abide in the Lord in your suffering.

Sometimes God allows us to struggle because he knows if the roots of our faith stay shallow, we'll never survive the storms ahead. Sometimes he allows it in order to draw us closer to himself, to teach us more about who he is and how he loves us. So my encouragement is this: simply spend time with the Vine Keeper, in both hard seasons and easy ones. Call on him to deepen your roots in the mighty ways only he can. Ask him to show you more of his all-powerful yet so personal self. That way when storms do come, you will not only survive; you can spiritually thrive.

PRUNING BACK THE WEAK SPOTS

Even when we accept that suffering can enrich our lives when we are rooted in faith, there is still the bold-faced fact that suffering hurts. We hate it, and we avoid it, and we pray against it for very good, very human reasons. Allowing suffering, we think, is not how a good God should operate! If he is truly a God of love, mercy, and kindness, if he is really a God who can do immeasurably more than I can ask or imagine (Ephesians 3:20), why didn't he intercede for me? Why didn't he heal Ben's brain or keep him from falling altogether? Why should I have to hurt this badly to grow into who the Lord is calling me to be? Why should I pray for healing and recovery when I've seen firsthand that those prayers might go unanswered? Should I even pray for physical healing, or should I simply ask for peace and comfort for those about to draw the divine short stick?

That last question really plagued me. Why are some pleas for healing granted and some dismissed? If God has already chosen whether or not to save a life, why even pray? I asked my pastor this very question a few weeks after Ben passed, when I heard of a childhood friend suffering from a similar brain injury. I wanted to pray for her. I wanted to call to account God's promise that if we ask, we will receive, that if we knock, the door will be opened (Matthew 7:7). But I did that with Ben, and nothing happened. Why didn't God show up?

Our prayers and singing for Ben in the hospital were nothing but well intended, but they also exposed a weak spot on my faith branches that needed to be sheared away. I was operating out of a mindset where if I could do enough, God would do the miracle. If I acted boldly and spoke faithfully and didn't doubt, he would heal Ben. And the truth is, he could have. But the harder truth is that we have a tendency to deal with God as a transactional God, especially in the midst of need or crisis. We can't help but think, *If I do what he commands, he will grant me what I'm asking.*

Sometimes he does. Sometimes he doesn't. There is great risk to our understanding of God, and ultimately to our accepting and trusting his sovereignty, when we engage with him in this way. It's very clear in Scripture that there is not a one-to-one ratio between our behavior and his blessing: "For he makes his sun rise on the evil and on the good, and sends rain on the just and on the unjust" (Matthew 5:45).

Before losing Ben, this idea of a transactional God was comfortable to me. I was generally pretty good, so my life had played out generally pretty well. I had to take a hard look inside to accept I could never do enough to get from God what I wanted. Pruning this idea from the branches of my faith was painful.

It feels frustrating when you see others who don't go all out in faith, or even have faith at all, receive a blessing that you don't. But in the wake of this pruning, I was reminded that a transactional God is not the kind of God I want to follow. Because if I got the one-to-one ratio I deserved—if my behavior was matched by his blessings—I could never do enough to merit his favor. I would never be seen as righteous in his eyes. I could never spend eternity with him. Without Jesus, who took the punishment I deserve for my lifetime of sin, I would never be right with God or experience his abundant grace.

It's not fair that I lost Ben the way I did. But it's also not fair that, through Jesus, God pours out unending grace and forgiveness over me every single time I sin and fall short. Grace isn't fair; it's a gift: "For by grace you have been saved through faith. And this is not your own doing; it is the gift of God" (Ephesians 2:8).

To put it bluntly, we deserve nothing but condemnation from God, yet by grace he offers us everything. The purpose of obedience to the Lord and his laws is not to earn his favor but to remind us of our desperate need for it. Similarly, the purpose of prayer is not to cash in faithful behavior for a desired outcome but to confide in a God who longs to connect with us and bring us comfort.

Blessed be the God and Father of our Lord Jesus Christ, the Father of mercies and God of all comfort, who comforts us in all our affliction, so that we may be able to comfort those who are in any affliction, with the comfort with which we ourselves are comforted by God. (2 Corinthians 1:3–4)

So, why should I pray for healing and recovery when I've seen firsthand that those prayers might go unanswered? Should I pray for physical healing, or should I simply ask for peace and comfort for those in pain?

Scripture tells us, "In everything by prayer and supplication with thanksgiving let your requests be made known to God" (Philippians 4:6). It also tells us, "Since we have such a hope [in Christ], we are very bold" (2 Corinthians 3:12) and that "nothing will be impossible with God" (Luke 1:37).

A big God can handle big prayers. If we believe in an almighty, all-powerful God, which I do, we are selling ourselves short and underestimating his divine nature when we don't pray bold prayers for healing. But if we don't couple his ability to answer our prayers with his authority to choose how he will do so, we diminish who he is as Lord and are left, at best, disappointed and, at worst, determined he can't be as good as he says he is.

When I addressed this struggle with my pastor—who wasn't at all taken aback by it—he kindly and compassionately directed me back to Jesus, who also begged the Lord for another way out. Even the Savior of the universe pled for a less brutal ending to his earthly story in the garden of Gethsemane before his death (Matthew 26:39, 42). Yet he asked it all with the humble caveat of "your will be done."

When you pray and bring your requests to God, don't hold back. Don't pare them down to something you think he'll grant so you don't end up disappointed. But also remember, as you lay your needs at his feet, his ways are higher than our ways (Isaiah 55:9); he doesn't owe you a transactional blessing; and at the end of the day, real trust sounds like, "I know you can, Father. I claim the miracle, but your will be done."

It wasn't a quick process for me to trust prayer again, to believe the words I prayed had power, to know the Lord heard them and held them in his heart even if they didn't give me the miracle I was begging for. God has all-powerful potential to heal the way we want him to heal, and sometimes he does. But other times what we ask of him is answered in ways that heal for eternity yet hurt deeply in the now (Revelation 21:4); ways that, if we're honest, feel more like a secondhand stone from our Father than a loaf of bread (Matthew 7:9).

Ben is now healed and whole, exactly as we pled at his bedside for him to be. God didn't deliver Ben back into my arms; he delivered Ben into his own. But the prayer he answered in eternal ways left me feeling unheard and alone in the now. I couldn't help but feel disappointed. Let down. Betrayed. A *lot* of us feel this way. We trust God to bring our good and his glory (Romans 8:28), so when the good and glory look, from where we stand, more like suffering and silence, we can't help but wonder or resent or despair. But anger and doubt don't undermine faith; they make it real. You don't have to hold back with God. You don't have to act like the things he prunes away in suffering don't hurt. He won't abandon you for your unrestrained disappointment. He will show up right in the middle of it and hold you while you kick and scream and cry.

It's okay to lament when we don't get the miracles we ask for. God knows that his answers to our prayers can break our hearts and taste like lemons. But there is no less love from our Father in the sourness and the pruning than there is in the moments of sweetness and pleasure. He is no less powerful, nor any less good, just because we don't like the way he answers our prayers. Whatever you do, don't stop running to him. Don't stop calling out to him and camping out on his throne of grace, because even if his answer is no, he can absolutely heal in spirit what he chooses not to heal in the flesh.

And when it hurts to admit he is good in spite of letting your worst nightmare come true, I'd encourage you to look to Jesus. The living, breathing, human Jesus who chose to unjustly suffer so that we could be justified and redeemed. The prophet Isaiah described him as "a man of sorrows and acquainted with grief," and he is often referred to as the Suffering Servant (Isaiah 53:3). Jesus is the one who willingly endured every hurt and sorrow in his earthly life that we will face in ours. He's the ultimate "high priest," Hebrews tells us, one who is not "unable to sympathize with our weaknesses" (4:14–15) because he is fully God yet also fully man. He came to suffer in our place, on our behalf, so that he would never ask us to face something he hadn't faced and conquered himself.

We may never get an explanation as to why a wholly good and sovereign God allows our suffering. We may never understand. But our healing begins when we choose trust over understanding.

Did God cause Ben's death, or did he permit an accident to happen in a dangerous, broken world? I've asked him. I've wept and yelled and pled and strained to hear an answer. But I don't need to know anymore. Ben is gone either way. I still hurt either way, and the Lord continues to faithfully walk with me either way. A good and loving Father whose desire is your faithful capacity to persevere doesn't take the lemons away. A vintner whose ultimate goal is the most beautiful, complex, rich wine plants the fruit on rocks and prunes back its branches. You may not understand your

Vintner's painful methods, but you can choose to trust that his purpose is for your ultimate good and his glory.

This doesn't mean God is indifferent to or doesn't hurt over our struggles. Just as he wept at his friend Lazarus's death (John 11:17–35), so Jesus weeps for our pain. The Father's promises to Joshua and Solomon and so many more in Scripture are the same promises he makes to us. He will never leave us or forsake us (Deuteronomy 31:8), and he will be with us always (1 Chronicles 28:20). He doesn't promise that he will fix us or our circumstances but that he will never leave us when we are too unfixed to fix ourselves.

The glory of the good news is that these sufferings, barren soils, and seasons full of lemons don't have to defeat us. Nor is it up to us to defeat them. The Lord promises, "We are more than conquerors through [Christ] who loved us" (Romans 8:37). This battle you're facing is one you cannot win alone. It's not up to you to conquer grief, loss, or suffering. It's not up to you to understand God's ways or what he permits and what he doesn't. It's not up to you to nourish your own roots or prune your own branches. When we rely on the Lord as the branch relies on the vine, only then can we endure and eventually flourish in the rocky soil.

We will ultimately conquer this world through Christ, along with all its hurt, loss, sorrow, and evil. The outcome has already been decided. It's not our responsibility. Praise Jesus, we are more than conquerors! We are "heirs of God and fellow heirs with Christ" (Romans 8:17), and glorious grapevines for the kingdom—vines that, through hardship, accrue depth, dimension, perseverance, and character. Until we suffer and endure the strains of this world, we remain on comfortable soil, with bushy branches and baby roots. It's not that the Lord wants us to suffer but that he cares more about the depth of our character than our temporary comforts.

He wants us to choose trust over understanding. He wants us to know him intimately, even when we don't know what he's doing. If we actively abide in him, we will be more radiant people with stronger faith than we knew we could be. We are becoming more and more like Christ as we struggle. We are sitting on a hillside, in rocky, barren soil, with a Vine Keeper who holds perfect, eternal control and whose painful work on the branches of our souls will yield a rich, fine wine—if we let it.

eight

HEAD UP, HANDS OFF

HOW DO I ACCEPT THE LOSS?

Hear the voice of my pleas for mercy,
     when I cry to you for help,
when I lift up my hands
     toward your most holy sanctuary.

PSALM 28:2

Acceptance is the one step in the five clinical stages of grief that felt impossible to me. Denial, depression, even bargaining seemed to take their places at different times on different days. Anger, though rare, certainly reared its head in moments as well. But I remember sitting on my counselor's deep-cushioned couch, staring at the word *acceptance* written on her whiteboard and thinking, *Impossible.*

It seemed so final. So permanent. Like giving up my will to fight in the bloodiest battle I'd ever endured. I rarely concede, and I hate the idea of throwing in the towel. It feels so unnatural not only because it is grossly incompatible with our culture but also because it seems like a personal affront to my strength and fortitude and ability to survive. We live in a white-knuckle world with white-flag disdain. Surrender is weakness, defeat, and vulnerability. Surrender meant admitting that Ben was really gone.

But in the wake of any kind of loss, we must eventually accept what we can't change or control. We do this by consciously putting our pain in the hands of the Savior.

You see, in the kingdom of God, submission is gloriously upside down. Getting low actually lifts you up. The power of surrender in Christ comes from knowing the one who has already laid everything down. Surrender takes every ounce of burden off of us. Death + Jesus = life. Sin + Jesus = salvation. Heartbreak + Jesus = restoration. And our job is to give it all to him and get out of the way. Our job is to stop trying and keep trusting. Our job is to believe Jesus when he said, "It is finished," even though we're stuck in a nightmare that feels like it will never end (John 19:30).

Jesus said, "If you cling to your life, you will lose it; but if you give up your life for me, you will find it" (Matthew 10:39 NLT). This was a tough truth for me to face—a difficult command in and of itself but unfathomable in the midst of grieving my husband. It wasn't the answer I wanted. It also isn't the answer the world gives. Jesus doesn't tell me to fight harder or stay busy; he tells me to give my sorrow to him and be still. Give him the hurt, the questions, the fear, and watch him work. But as the days slipped further and further from my last with Ben and everyone else's lives marched on, I felt as though my only hope was to hold tighter, to cling with everything I had, so the world wouldn't forget his memory and time wouldn't continue widening the gap between us. I'd convinced myself that maybe if I held on tight enough, if I kept my life just how it was before the day he died, I might be okay.

The first thing I had to surrender was the grief itself. I thought I had. My prayers and Instagram posts and coffee conversations with people said I had. I truly was doing the best I could, and I continued to praise God along the way. But as hard as I tried, I made plenty of mistakes. The world kept praising me for how well I was handling everything, but behind those praises, I felt like a fraud. I knew all the moments I'd snapped and yelled at my parents or sisters for no reason. I knew the nights I'd drunk myself to sleep because I was afraid to lie awake again in our bed alone. I knew all the people I'd avoided or lied to, pretending I didn't get their messages because I felt too depleted to talk. I knew the ways and occasions I had handled grieving far from well, and they burdened me. That behavior wasn't who I wanted to be, and it wasn't helpful. My deep, unaddressed pain was, as my therapist put it, "coming out sideways."

On top of the shame I was feeling because of these sideways behaviors, grief had also totally ransomed my memory. No matter how much I strained to remember or how reflective I was, my mind seemed to have taken a complete sabbatical. I simply couldn't remember things! I couldn't remember times Ben and I had shared, things he'd said, even intimate physical details about him. It was like my hard drive had been erased. I felt captive to my grief and frustrated that it seemed to be getting the better of me.

Then one bitter December day, I went to see my therapist. I shared with her about my struggle to remember and the regrettable "sideways" reactions.

I kept staring at the whiteboard and at that word: *acceptance.* I couldn't imagine accepting everything that had happened, but even more than that, I didn't want to accept that I had, at times, handled my hurt so poorly. I blamed myself for making mistakes and looking so faithful to the world when I'd failed on many occasions. I'd thought I was doing well, but maybe I couldn't handle grief as well as I thought I could.

I started to cry with frustration, eyes on the floor. Then my counselor asked me two questions: "What would Ben say to you?" and "What would Jesus say to you?"

I exhaled. I had a thousand things I wanted to say to myself that weren't helpful, but I knew in an instant what the two loves of my life would say to me. Ben would say, "Bug, I'm so proud of you." He was such a champion of my successes and the ultimate forgiver of my failures. And were he here to witness me grappling with grief, his answer wouldn't have been any different. Ben would have been proud of me for the days I'd praised God and would have given me a place to rest and receive grace on the days I fell short.

And Jesus? Jesus would say, "I've borne all of this for you already—the pain, the loss, the sorrow, the sin. Stop trying to bear it yourself."

A flood of relief washed over me in ways that felt almost physical, like an actual yoke being lifted off of me. And in that moment it struck me: "Head up, hands off." I guess without thinking I blurted it out loud.

"I'm sorry?" my therapist asked.

"Head up, hands off," I whispered and looked up straight at her. "I can't do this myself."

With the hypothetical but oh-so-real answers to these two

simple questions, I felt as though the weight of the world had been lifted from me. For the rest of our time that day, we talked about how neither Ben nor God was disappointed with how I grieved. We pictured and narrated scenes of me physically handing my grief over to Jesus. We worked through the truth that grief wasn't something I could handle alone and that having grace for myself and remembering the Lord's grace for me was the only way to get through. Grace for ourselves and from others is absolutely pivotal as we grieve.

After that meeting, I finally surrendered. I told the Lord that I accepted that I couldn't endure grieving Ben with my own strength, but that with Jesus' power and grace, I could. Not only did I feel a huge sense of relief (this wasn't all on me!), but later that very day, the memories that had up until then been captured by grief flooded back. Moments and scenes that my brain had frozen in trauma were gloriously relinquished and ran like the most life-giving slideshow through my mind, one after the other.

I love the way C. S. Lewis captured this most merciful phenomenon after losing his wife in *A Grief Observed*:

> And suddenly at the very moment when, so far, I mourned H. least, I remembered her best. Indeed it was something (almost) better than memory; an instantaneous, unanswerable impression. To say it was like a meeting would be going too far. Yet there was that in it which tempts one to use those words. It was as if the lifting of the sorrow removed a barrier.[1]

The lifting of the sorrow, the acceptance that grief is something so out of my human control, removed a barrier. It restored memory and love and life.

Since then I often feel Ben's presence—not in celestial, strumming-a-harp-on-a-cloud ways but in moments where the closeness of his character caresses the simple movements of my day: his sheer joy for the sunshine, his laugh at the ridiculous, even his protection in moments I feel afraid. The Lord gifted me a Ben-like filter through which to keep living, even if he's not in any more of the pictures. I now remember him more clearly than ever.

As the years since his passing have stretched on, I've learned what it means to concede as an act of trust, not an admission of defeat or failure. But hear me: surrender isn't a magic pill that takes the pain away. The pain is just as real, and the wounds just as open, but through surrender, real healing can begin.

When I quit trying to resist how deeply I was broken and accepted that all I'd lost was safe in God's hands, my healing was no longer dependent on what I could do or how strong I could be. My healing was now in the hands of the one who makes mountains out of mustard seeds, wine out of water, and beauty out of ashes. When I began to stand on the truth that only Jesus could restore and resurrect my heart and my life into something new, something stronger than before, I started to live again.

Surrender isn't easy, and it's also not a one-time thing. It is turning my hands open and lifting my head up minute by minute, day by day, to the Lord. Only God can take something that feels like giving up and use it to bring back life, not in black and white but in full, abundant, vibrant color. That is my prayer for all of us: that we have the courage to face the pain head-on and the faith to take our hands off the hurt and lift our heads up to the Healer. Because when we do that, he will help us accept the devastation of what we've lost, and he will begin to set us free from the sorrow that is keeping us captive.

My healing was
now in the hands
of the one who
makes mountains
out of mustard
seeds, wine out of
water, and beauty
out of ashes.

———

GIVING THE GIFT BACK TO THE GIVER

In addition to surrendering the actual process of grieving, I also had to lay down the incredible gift I'd lost. I've been cautioned before with the warning not to love the gift more than the Giver—you know, when we claim we love God but what we actually love most about him is our health, wealth, and the slew of blessings that come from his hand.

This is so natural, so human, yet so chock-full of potential for distrusting and resenting the God who gives us the gifts in the first place. We see it clearly in children. A child loves Mommy and snuggles Mommy and trusts Mommy has just what she needs until Mommy takes away her toys. Does she really love the toy more than her mother, or does she feel betrayed by a mom who takes away her toys at bedtime?

It's hard to trust Mom when she takes away something that's right in front of us that makes us feel good and happy. Mom gave us the toys to begin with, so it's natural to feel double-crossed when she takes them away.

My mom explained it best a few weeks after Ben passed: "It's as if I was just betrayed by my very best friend. I trusted my Father for a miracle, and when he didn't deliver, I felt like, 'Were you ever there at all?'"

Betrayed by a very best friend. Let down by a Father. These things are a breeding ground for heartbreak and, ultimately, distrust. Though we don't always have the words to articulate it, feeling this overwhelming letdown by God is a normal response to suffering. In fact, in the very admission of our disappointment, we aren't abandoning our faith; rather, we are affirming the depth of our trust in him to begin with.

My mother is one of the most ardently faithful women I know. Her anger, her honesty, her lament in what felt like a breach of trust from her heavenly Father didn't threaten her faith. Her struggle actually enriched it with every tearful step she took back into his arms. Even though she felt betrayed, she was faithful to surrender her broken heart back to the one who broke it. She chose to trust even when she didn't understand.

It's okay to throw the temper tantrum. It's okay to question when God takes from us what brings us such happiness. It's okay that we can't understand why he took it away. Because at the end of the day, he is still here to embrace us and sustain us and collect our tears (Psalm 56:8). He is our ultimate comforter (2 Corinthians 1:3–4).

But we must stop fighting him and expecting him to cater to our every want and desire, and simply let him hold us. We must surrender our anger with the situation so we can find our way back to trust in the Savior. We must pray and expectantly wait for the courage to love the Giver more than the gift. There is no harder nor more necessary space in which to reorder our loves than in the loss of someone we cherish. In order to accept that God is good even when he allows us to suffer, we must learn to surrender the one we lost to the Creator who gifted that person to us in the first place. As C. S. Lewis explained, "What St. Paul says ['Do not mourn like those that have no hope'] can comfort only those who love God better than the dead, and the dead better than themselves."[2]

The latter part of this—the idea of loving the dead better than myself—came naturally for me. As one of the most deeply joyful, content, and abundantly loving men I've known, Ben was made for heaven. We all are, of course, but the way he lived his life and loved his people make it so easy to picture him with Jesus and other friends and family, reveling in all the excitement and energy and connection of eternity. No one deserved a go-to-heaven-early pass more than Ben Selecman.

The part about loving God more than loving him was a whole different story. I struggled with that idea for many months—and felt profoundly ashamed about it too. I've always known God, believed in God, talked with God. Christ truly was the cornerstone for our marriage. But when the greatest earthly gift God had given me was taken away, I was left to face a harsh reality: Had I loved my life, my marriage, my dreams, my husband—you name it—more than I had actually loved the person of Jesus? Like Job when his cherished blessings were taken without apology, would I continue to trust, or would I revert to his wife's approach of "curse God and die" (Job 2:9)?

For me, surrendering to God's sovereignty *and* his goodness, in spite of the fact that I felt betrayed by him, was crucial to accepting all I'd lost. And though I did so reluctantly at first, I asked the Lord to help me love him more than I love Ben. To value the Giver more than the gift. It doesn't mean I love Ben any less; in fact, I love him more now than I ever have. But in surrendering the greatest gift of my life back to the Giver who also took him away, my loves began to reorder. I began to hand Ben back over to his heavenly Father and accept the Father's handiwork in me. I had to lay down the gift of our marriage in order to accept that God truly is good and trustworthy. And like the mom taking the toys away, not for a second does our God love us less because we don't like him in the moment. He cherishes every fiber of our fragile, weary beings.

Run to him. Surrender all of your gifts and grievances to him, and he will reveal to you the absolute greatest gift of all: himself.

LITTLE FUNERALS FOR MY FUTURE

It took many tearful months and brutally honest prayers to take my hands off my grief and the gift of Ben and our marriage. Everything in this fallen world is temporary. We will say goodbye to endless people and places, seasons and opportunities, good things and bad as we experience life. I believe accepting these goodbyes is one of the greatest challenges we face as humans. In fact, unwelcome goodbyes can be so heartbreaking and disorienting that author and teacher Lysa TerKeurst refers to the idea as "little funerals." She wrote this on her Facebook page in 2019 to promote her book *It's Not Supposed to Be This Way*:

> But in the midst of my own heartbreaking realities, I realized I needed to start having little funerals for the ways I thought my life would turn out.
>
> Sometimes to get life back, you have to face the death of what you thought your life would look like. You have to let go of what isn't so that you can grab hold of what can be. Letting go of these expectations isn't an end. It's often what must be present for the brand new to begin.[3]

Truth be told, when I read about Lysa's little-funerals principle after Ben died, absolutely nothing about the idea sunk in. In fact, I rejected it. What the hell was a little funeral, and why should I suffer through little funerals when I'd just endured one of epic proportions?

And where does one get off describing any funeral as "little"? Funerals are an unwelcome, unwilling admission of the death of someone who was deeply part of who we are. Nothing about death is little. Funerals of every sort are a reminder that this life flat-out isn't what we desire it to be. Funerals are big, and I didn't want to suffer through any more of them.

Maybe I could lay down what had happened, and maybe I could surrender Ben back to the Lord who had created him in the first place. But what terrified me to think about, much less have a little funeral for and surrender to a God who had just proved himself wildly unpredictable, was my future.

One of my greatest fears since the day Ben died remains as I write these words right now: How will I love Ben and love someone else? How can I let someone else in without pushing Ben out? How can I fully embrace a new love yet face the fear of a new love taking the old one's place? How do I show up fully vulnerable, afraid, and honest with a new partner when the fingerprints of my first one are still all over my life?

I don't know these answers yet, but I've prayed nearly every day since Ben's passing that my day for new love will come. I don't know how or when the Lord will work in my heart to make space for an old love and a new one. But I do know my only responsibility is to give both my fears and my desires to God daily and wait expectantly as he does the rest. It's my responsibility to accept and acknowledge the little funeral for the future I'd planned and to lay down my questions at my Father's feet.

This doesn't mean valuing the gifts I ask of him for my future more than I value the Giver. It means I come to him without any filter, bringing my whole hurt and my whole heart. It means taking my hands off the desire to be a wife and a mom and lifting my head up to the one whom I will persistently ask to provide those things for me. For me, surrendering my marriage to Ben and my longing to marry again looks like this:

Father, I still don't understand why you'd give me the desire of my heart and take it away. But I am forever thankful for the gift of Ben and his love. I'm thankful for the time you did give me with him. But you also know how much I long to have great love again. You know more than anything I want to raise children to love you and walk with you. You know I want all of these things, and like the persistent widow (Luke 18:1–8), I'll never stop asking you for them. But I want them in your way, in your will, in your timing. I trust you. I give them to you. Thank you for sowing more trust and patience and contentment in me as I wait.

This is raw, honest, surrendered prayer. I struggle to say these words sometimes, but for me, they are what acceptance and trust look like. And I think this is what Jesus was getting at when he told us to pick up our crosses and follow him.

Then Jesus told his disciples, "If anyone would come after me, let him deny himself and take up his cross and follow me. For whoever would save his life will lose it, but whoever loses his life for my sake will find it." (Matthew 16:24–25)

I can't be the only one who glosses over this awful instruction, can I? I mean, I get the idea—our sacrifices in following Christ are nothing compared to his sacrifice to die for us on the cross, save us, and make us right with God. There will be things we're called to give up or turn away from in order to walk closer with the Lord. But why did my cross have to be Ben-sized? Why couldn't it have been bypassing a job opportunity or being called to missions somewhere I didn't want to go? Why did I have to lose my marriage in order to walk into the life Christ wants me to lead?

I'd already laid Ben's life down, literally; why did I keep having to lay down all these parts of mine? If I'm honest with myself, Jesus' call for me to bear this widow cross still feels unfair, even cruel. Why me? I may never know.

What I do know is that just like the physical cross Jesus carried and died on for our sake, the Lord often uses what feels cruel in our lives to cultivate our character. Jesus' life was defined by unfair suffering and sacrifice, and the crosses we bear and the little funerals we suffer are often what God uses to refine us and make us more like Christ. Second Corinthians tells us that we are "always being given over to death for Jesus' sake, so that the life of Jesus also may be manifested in our mortal flesh" (4:11) and are "being transformed into [his] same image from one degree of glory to another" (3:18).

I wish the relationship between struggle and sanctification (the act of God refining us spiritually) wasn't so close. But we see through the life of Jesus and so many of his followers that suffering leads to greater Christlikeness. If our desire is to grow deeper in relationship with him, hardship is often part of our journeys. And with hardship inevitably comes little funerals of how we planned for our lives to be. Surrendering our losses and gifts and futures to God won't feel good, but it will allow him to start shaping us into fuller, richer versions of ourselves.

The Lord winces each time he watches us live out another little funeral. He hurts for us, his beloved children, when we must engage a new battle with grief and give up another piece of what we wanted our lives to look like. But he also smiles because he knows we are being reshaped, restored, and reworked into something even more resilient and beautiful. His crosses are not cruel; he calls us to carry them because he can see the splendor that's waiting for us on the other side.

We will face a lifetime of little funerals as we say goodbye to people, places, and things we hold dear. Please, dear friends, don't try to carry these burdens and face these little funerals alone. Let your friends sit with you and cry with you and encourage you as you accept the things you wish desperately weren't true. Let the Lord in on how angry you are that you have to go through giving up beloved parts of your life over and over again, and lay your hurt at his feet. He is merciful. And while he won't take away the crosses we bear, he will always help us carry them.

As I look back over the years following Ben's death, I see now that though my head resisted the idea of little funerals, my heart was practicing them all along. I had to surrender the lie that I could handle my grief in my own strength. I had to lay down my pride and my desire to understand. I had to accept the loss of a marriage, and with it, parts of my identity I couldn't get back. The list goes on and on. With each new hurdle I faced, whether a mountain or a molehill, the Lord set the stage for one more little funeral. And you know what? In the wake of those little funerals—in the aftermath of accepting the most painful parts of my loss and my story—I have found the greatest strength and most palpable hope.

From our earthly perspective surrender exposes fragility, but from a heavenly perspective, it assures security. The Lord's most triumphant moments come in easing his children's brokenness—children who surrender their vain attempts to heal themselves to the one who makes all things new. We've been seeing surrender from the wrong perspective. Worldly surrender concedes defeat; biblical surrender heralds hope. What feels to us like accepting despair in the darkness is, in reality, getting out of God's way so he can usher in the light!

His mercies are new every morning (Lamentations 3:22–23), and praise God because those little funerals need big mercies to be endured! Each day when my feet hit the floor, I cling to the promise that Christ can meet my every need in the upcoming twenty-four hours. His abundant mercy is enough to sustain me one day at a time. It's enough on the days when normal feels impossible. It's enough on the days when I feel so far from who I used to be that I wonder if I'll ever know who I am again. It's enough on the days when I'm on my knees, tears streaming, begging God to assure me I'll get to love someone again.

Surrender your grief, your gifts, your future, and everything you're struggling to accept to the Lord. Lay them down every day, one at a time. Write them on a slip of paper to keep in your Bible or on your bedside, so that even on the days when you feel like you can't, you concede them anyway. They are much safer in the Lord's hands than in your own.

nine

ROOTS AND WINGS

HOW DO I MOVE FORWARD?

> Therefore, if anyone is in Christ, he
> is a new creation. The old has passed
> away; behold, the new has come.
>
> 2 CORINTHIANS 5:17

We are a culture of power-throughers. We champion progress and tenacity and self-reliance. We rally around those who refuse to crumble under pressure. And in many facets of life, those traits are admirable. They can help us succeed. Where they do not serve us well is in seasons of grief. We've already talked about the power of surrender in accepting whatever suffering may befall us.

But as we continue to surrender our grief, our gifts, and our futures, how do we move forward?

This is what everyone wants for us, isn't it? For us to *move on, move forward, start fresh*—whatever verbiage you want to use. Those who love us long to see us spring into new life and no longer stay stuck in the throes of our pain. And in a lot of ways, we want that too. I longed for a day when the start of each new month wouldn't hurl me back into the trauma of Ben's days in the hospital. For a while the first day of every month seemed to reset a sort of internal clock—a solemn, resounding tick as each day of Ben's twelve spent in the ICU replayed in my mind. It haunted me and stole nearly all focus and energy from my days. As the date approached, my anxiety returned, and I was left emotionally paralyzed all over again. Would I ever move forward from this cruel montage of memories? Is it really possible to move on from feeling engulfed in pain? And, if it is, how do we do it?

Time passed certainly plays a benevolent role in softening memories' edges, but the process of progress also takes hard work. In my case, the work was brainspotting, a method of processing trauma that required me to thrust my heart right back into the scene that broke it. I had to embrace the pain, not combat it. It's work that works, but it totally sucks.

I cannot say strongly enough how important professional counseling has been to my grieving process. It was a huge part of my healing, and I encourage anyone who is struggling to pursue wise, professional counsel if they are able to do so.

Even so, therapy is not the only way to move forward. A dear friend of mine who also lost her husband in her twenties gave me some profound advice that took me a while to make sense of. She told me the only way she found to keep living with any sort of joy after her Davey's death was to "make friends with her grief." She didn't wallow in it or, on the other hand, write off any of the pain it continued to inflict, but she awoke to the reality that it would never fully go away. She learned that in order to move forward with her life, she must live *with* her grief and stop struggling to live in spite of it.

My counselor gave an apt analogy for this idea. She assured me that with time, work, and faith, we could take the grief from the windshield of my world to the side mirrors, and eventually, to the rearview mirror. We could never fully expel it from the car, but then again, why would I want to? Expelling would mean forgetting. That would be the greatest loss of all. I don't think I'm quite to the rearview yet, but the Lord has certainly defrosted my front windshield.

It's important to remember, the process of grieving is just that—a process. It takes time for the ice to melt. It takes time to make friends with your grief and learn how to interact with your pain. But just as my counselor assured me, let me encourage you: your pain will eventually make its way to the rearview mirror. The loss won't always be the only thing you can see. Though you hate that you have to grieve at all, you can learn to live side by side with the sadness rather than head-to-head with it. You don't have to power through or muscle up to survive. You can let yourself fully lament at the same time you take brave steps to move forward.

CRY THE UGLY CRY

Valentine's Day was not a holiday Ben and I typically gave much weight to, but it ended up being one that helped me learn to better engage with my grief. Just two days prior had been five months since his passing. I'd done fairly well this fifth go-round, the replay of the twelve days of his hospitalization feeling a little less like HD trauma and a little more like sepia-toned scenes.

I was fiddling around in the kitchen, making coffee and trying to distract myself with mindless chores. I didn't expect that day to hurt as badly as Thanksgiving and Christmas had, since this holiday wasn't special to us; still, busy was better than having a breakdown, so fiddle I did. After I finished my coffee and cleaned up the kitchen, I sat down and pulled out my phone. Was this a good idea? Would every photo on my feed today be happy "my forever Valentine" posts that would make me feel all the more alone? I decided against it.

Instead I dug through the closet in my office, where I keep most of my "Ben things"—our marriage license, our wedding video, his passport and Social Security card, you name it. I hadn't pulled out much of it up to this point, but something about today felt like a good time. I rummaged through his wallet, pulling out friends' old business cards that he had no doubt proudly shared with whomever he met. I read old Post-it notes he'd written me and left on my bedside table. I flipped through photos, still mostly holding it together, until I found one that I hadn't remembered seeing before.

It was a beautiful black-and-white picture from our wedding ceremony. It must have been taken during a prayer because both our heads are bowed, and our eyes are closed. It's not a well-framed shot—the preacher's back is blocking half the photo—but even in the middle of a prayer, we were clearly squeezing each other's hands tightly, both of us grinning from ear to ear like kids on Christmas morning. We were so overwhelmingly in love.

That photo sent my mind reeling—not over the accident or the hospital or all the things I'd been trying to move on from thinking about every month, but into a whirlwind of remembering who Ben was and how desperately I missed him. I knelt down in the closet and sobbed. I clutched the photo and the worn-out wallet and the Post-its and wailed a truly ugly cry. *Is this what it means to "lean into" my grief?* If so, leaning in felt more like jumping from a plane with no parachute.

Up to that point, I'd gritted my way through all the things. Sorted and packaged most of his stuff, sold his truck, fixed the credit cards and bank accounts. I'd also started to learn and apply many of the good outlets for my pain. My work, journaling, nature, time with my compassionate community of friends and family who buoyed me daily—they had all been integral parts of navigating life without Ben.

But what I failed to understand was that, though I'd begun taking healthy steps to mend what was broken, I was grieving with my guard up. I was praying and clinging to Scripture, even writing blog posts sharing my grief in hopes of encouraging others, not just to temper my pain but to avoid at all costs feeling it in full. I longed for the Lord to use my walk to heal others, and he has, thanks to NaSHEville and the voice he gave me to speak life into other widows. But for a while, I was working to help heal in others what I hadn't yet allowed the Lord to fully heal in me. I needed to stop resisting the full emotional impact of my pain in order to start living purposefully within it.

Something about that photo broke me in ways I hadn't broken down before. Pain flooded fully and wholly in. No more powering through. I had surrendered and accepted losing Ben, but now I simply missed him. I was still so in love with a man who was no longer here. I felt pure sadness, overwhelming lament. I don't think I'd understood the real meaning of *lamenting* before.

So I called out that emptiness. I faced the huge Ben-shaped hole that I had no idea how to fill, and I sobbed for him. Grief went from something I was processing to someone I was pining for. I longed for Ben with deep, guttural hurt.

This, I believe, is what true lament looks like. It looks like letting yourself break into a million pieces and fully embracing your sorrow so that it can no longer hold you captive. You can be free to move forward without fear of forgetting what you're leaving behind, but not until you stop resisting feeling the weight of your whole pain.

I yearned for Ben's boyish smile, for his morning prayers and evening cocktails. For the way his shoulders had enough muscle to cradle my head at night but not so much it smashed my earring back into the side of my face. For the way he never, ever finished a whole granola bar and would always toss me the last bite. I longed for all the anomalies and quirks and laughable flaws the world lost on the day he left. They seemed the only things in all creation that could glue my broken heart back together. I even wondered how the Lord would mend it back without those bits of Ben's character to fill in the jagged gaps.

I love what Lysa TerKeurst says about breaking down to move forward in her book *It's Not Supposed to Be This Way*: "We think the shattering in our lives could not possibly be for any good. But what if shattering is the only way to get dust back to its basic form so that something new can be made?"[1]

She, too, faced a season of devastating suffering, and like me, she learned firsthand what it's like to shatter, to face grief head-on and be left in a thousand pieces. The good news is that the Lord will use those pieces to shape us into something new, into people who have the courage to move forward because we've felt the full impact of what we've lost—and we've survived.

In Scripture, we see this same face-first breaking down and lamenting from King David. After the Lord told David that his son would surely die, David "fasted and went in and lay all night on the ground. And the elders of his house stood beside him, to raise him from the ground, but he would not, nor did he eat food with them" (2 Samuel 12:16–17).

Even before his son passed away, David let in his overwhelming grief and let his heart fully break. He fasted and fell to the ground. Emotional dust. Then, when his servants delivered the message that his son was indeed dead, "David arose from the earth and washed and anointed himself and changed his clothes. And he went into the house of the LORD and worshiped" (2 Samuel 12:20).

Though this may seem hasty or unrealistic to us—*How could he just get up and move on so quickly?*—this is exactly how the Lord wants us to face our sorrow. He wants us to lament and lay on the ground and break into pieces when our absolute worst nightmares come true. But he doesn't want us to stay dust. As the Lord did with David, molding him into an even more faithful and admirable king than he was at the time of his loss, God wants to shape us into stronger, more resilient souls. He wants us to keep living even when we're still in pieces.

In order to move forward, I had to first learn how to lament. I needed to admit how desperately I missed Ben. My grief had to become less of an enemy and more of an unsolicited companion. My options weren't to either resist the pain or be defeated by it. I didn't have to either wallow entirely or run away completely. I could miss Ben and move forward at the same time, forever.

ROOTS AND WINGS

That first Valentine's Day experience was crucial in setting the stage for me to grieve more fully and honestly. I felt I'd gotten permission to both reset for the future and continue remembering the past. For a long time, I was afraid that my progress would mean forgetting parts of Ben and our life together. But it doesn't! As unfathomable as it is to my finite mind and broken heart, I can continue to cherish our past and move toward my future. Or as Ben would quote from our favorite movie, *Sweet Home Alabama*, "You can have roots and wings, Mel."[2]

Nothing about God's work is accidental. We have two hands for a reason—one to hold what was and one to reach out toward what's to come. We have two hands that, when turned and open to the one who can fill them, can hold in the same moment all that we've lost and all that we long for. We can treasure the things and people we love that are no longer around, and we can find freedom in moving forward into new places the Lord has for us. We can take chances and take steps. We'll face welcome and unwelcome changes, both of which will feel scary and painful. But pray for the courage to embrace what's next, and trust your good Father to shepherd you through the opportunities in your path.

A major "roots and wings" moment for me was moving out of our home. Ben and I had bought what we'd intended to be our ten-year, start-a-family home just a few months before we married. It was the mark of a new beginning and the inception of some of our best conversations, meals, and memories. For a while after he passed, our home felt like my only place of real solace; the only place I could feel close to him and press pause on a life so suddenly snatched away. It was the most physical piece of us I had left.

But after a few months, my sanctuary began to feel more like a prison. I was forced to surrender the false hope that staying in our home might make the situation go away, or that all Ben's things being in their right place might actually bring him back. Leaving was the scariest choice I made in that first year. What if being somewhere different made me feel lonelier? If I packed up his things to move, would I have the strength to unpack them again? *Should* I unpack them again?

But my heart knew very well that hiding out in a still frame of our life wasn't going to keep my story from rolling forward. So I prayed, *Lord, if this isn't where I'm going to heal, take me somewhere else.* And on a cold, rainy morning, one where all I wanted was to curl up with Ben's flannel and pretend he was just out hunting, my real estate agent called. I was reluctant. I wanted to wallow in our life together, not get up and move on with mine alone.

But I went to check out the house, and like everything, it was a whirlwind of conflicting emotions. Part of me felt alive again, a spark of hope I didn't expect. Part of me felt like I was betraying Ben, taking an early checkout from the life we'd committed to. Part of me felt like I was moving too fast, like people would see it as running away. Part of me felt like I was free. And as he does, the Lord showed up on the day of my move with a faithful little God nod that this was exactly where I needed to be.

The daily devotional book *Jesus Calling,* which I've started my days with since 2008, featured these scriptures on January 27, 2019, and January 28, 2019—the day before and the morning of my leaving our home.

Trust in the LORD with all your heart,
 and do not lean on your own understanding.
In all your ways acknowledge him,
 and he will make straight your paths. (Proverbs 3:5–6)

"And behold, I am with you always, to the end of the age."
(Matthew 28:20)

The first is what Ben prayed for us and over us every day we were together. His mom even got this verse tattooed on her forearm on the first anniversary of his death. The second is the final assurance in Jesus' pep talk and Great Commission to the disciples. The Great Commission (Matthew 28:16–20) is the other passage that Ben prayed each day we were together—to make disciples. It's a big calling, but as God promises, he'll be with us always.

God shows up in these moments of change and courageous steps forward. He speaks intimately and clearly when we follow him into scary places. He whispers what only he could know we need to hear. Move into these places, not without fear but with eyes expectant to see and ears ready to hear how the Lord will cheer us on when we enter them bravely.

Moving into my new house became one of my greatest blessings. It was beautiful and bright, a literal clean slate on which the Lord began to paint fresh pictures of what my life could be. Not an empty, lonely life but a vibrant one that could be mine again. One of learning to be myself while grafting Ben's memories and deer mounts and past right into my future. One that overflowed with life rather than resounding of death.

These moments of embracing grief and moving forward are not all house-sized. In fact, many of them may seem like minutia to those around us. But do not undervalue them! It may be sorting your loved one's clothes or cancelling their credit cards. It may be taking on hobbies your loved one enjoyed—even if you didn't before—because now they feel good to do. It may be looking at old pictures that break your heart but let you feel your loved one's presence and remember them all the more closely. It may be replacing old pictures with new ones. Whatever unexpected invitations life and the Lord present to you, prayerfully consider them, and if you feel led, embrace them. They will be scary. They will hurt. They may leave you shattered and feeling like dust for a little while. But only when we fully embrace the pain and give our pieces to the Lord will we start to find the courage to move forward.

CHOOSE COMPASSION OVER COMPARISON

In the last chapter I shared some of my fears about finding love again as a young widow: How will I love Ben and love someone else? How can I let someone else in without pushing Ben out? How can I fully embrace a new love yet face the fear of a new love taking the old one's place? How do I show up fully vulnerable, afraid, and honest with a new partner when the fingerprints of my first one are still all over my life?

And while surrendering my anxiety around these questions requires continued prayer, I want to share with you what my slow movement back into the dating space has looked like.

My first date after Ben died was the night before my thirtieth birthday. I didn't plan it that way, though I will admit the timing felt reassuring. Here I was on the cusp of a new decade, and maybe this date was a reminder to me to keep holding out hope. Maybe it was proof that God *was* in perfect control of my future as I'd been claiming for almost two years at this point. Out of nowhere, a date fell into my lap!

I say out of nowhere because that's exactly how it happened. I got connected with this guy through a friend of a friend. People had their eyes peeled and feelers out there on my behalf, and that felt encouraging. Because I'd never met this person and we'd only exchanged a few texts, we decided just to meet for drinks. This way, I thought, it would be early in the evening. Plus it would be quick, and there would be less pressure than a full-on dinner.

Though grateful for a renewed sense of hope that there are still good, thirty-something-year-old men out there, I was nervous. I hadn't been on a first date in more than five years, and I hadn't been on a blind date ever. (To be fair, I'd seen a few pictures of this guy and had gotten a few key details, but nothing more.) I was anxious about my outfit, my hair, even his clothes and his hair. Would I be attracted to him? Would he be funny? Or at the very least able to roll with my sarcastic banter that tends to ramp up when I'm uncomfortable?

But more than any of those concerns, I was terrified to talk about Ben. I'd told my story a thousand times by that point—one-on-one with women, on podcasts, at events, on TV broadcasts, you name it. I had it down to a succinct summary because if I could control the conversation, I could control my emotions. If I decided when and how to share my most painful experience, and I appeared fine telling the story, maybe the listener would be fine hearing it too. I'd tell him quickly and painlessly so we could just move on without the awkwardness of how heavy my story is.

"I want to get it out of the way," I told my therapist the week before the date. And I felt good about that. No elephant in the room, no wondering if he knew or didn't know, no having to avoid certain topics where Ben might come up or leave him out of stories that he is actually a part of. Maybe this was how I'd move forward in the dating world. It was clear my therapist disagreed with my logic, encouraging me not to put a time stamp on sharing my story or rush through what was likely going to be hard on me emotionally. But that was my plan. The quicker the better.

So, I ended up giving this man my "well, I was married, and my husband died, but the Lord has been so good to me, and now I get to help widows through my work" elevator pitch as planned. And I was right about one thing: it was quick. But I was very wrong about another: sharing something that painful and vulnerable too soon doesn't get the elephant out of the room. It plops that awkward elephant right on top of your table. In retrospect it's clear to me this wasn't the right way to share something so tender, and I have since had to learn more patience and grace with myself.

Other than the rough I-lost-my-husband delivery, it was a fine date. By the end, it did feel a bit like an interview given all his questions, which may have been his attempt to stick to small talk after my overwhelming confession. He was kind and smart and very intentional to inquire about different parts of my life, but let's just call a spade a spade: he was boring. All I could think with each dry exchange was, *He's not Ben. No one ever will be Ben.*

Since then, I've had a few more first and second and third dates with different people—some equally as boring and some much more comfortable and fun. It's impossible to sit across from another man and not see the ways he falls short of the one I still love. It's natural to compare because Ben has set the bar in my mind. Even with men I did like and laugh with and get along with well, comparison seemed inevitable. I had to consciously work to just see the person in front of me and not make mental checks in the "like Ben" or "not like Ben" columns.

Most of you, widowed or not, know what this tendency to compare feels like, whether on a first date, at a new job, or simply in a new season. We are wired to measure A against B. But if we don't take control of the comparing, as I've had to in dating, we will miss the enjoyable parts of where we are because we're pitting it unfairly against where we've been.

It's been more than three years since my last date with Ben, and every time I get ready for a new one now, I have to pep-talk myself out of comparison to him and into compassion for me because that's what I deserve. Compassion is what we all deserve. I must remind myself it's okay that dating is difficult and emotionally confusing for me now. What matters is that I'm trying. Compassion!

I will love Ben until the day I die, just like I promised to do on our wedding day, but I truly believe God has made me capable of loving another fully too. I don't understand how yet because I haven't gotten there yet. It's hard to imagine. But I'm choosing compassion toward myself as I learn to date again because in self-compassion, I'm finding courage.

Don't hold yourself to impossible standards or expect the new person or new season to be just like the old. Similarity isn't necessarily equality, and difference isn't always less than. Losing a spouse, a loved one, or anything in this world that we care about leaves holes in the fabric of who we are. I believe a personal relationship with Jesus is the only thing that can fill those holes. If we try to force another person or thing to fill them, everyone involved will be disappointed. Though it's not easy, we can cherish what we had without comparing what's to come, and we can call on Jesus to fill the holes that no one else can.

Dating after all I've been through often leaves me frustrated, feeling like I'm back at the starting line of a race I thought I'd already finished. But it has also taught me much about perseverance. I have to keep praying, keep surrendering, and keep bravely embracing new, uncomfortable experiences. The only way to live a life of rich, sustaining hope in a world full of lemons on Friday is to persevere, one day at a time, not in your own strength but with the mighty power of the Holy Spirit in you.

Paul knew it. "Not only that, but we rejoice in our sufferings, knowing that suffering produces endurance, and endurance produces character, and character produces hope" (Romans 5:3–4). And I know it now more than ever. That, friends, is what this whole book is about—finding hope in the midst of heartbreak and allowing the Lord to sustain you and carry you forward.

You may be suffering greatly, but you don't have to stay stuck. The future is uncertain and scary, but you have a Good Shepherd to lead the way. Follow him. Trust him. Your healing and progress through grief will be painful. It won't look like a polished plan with a pretty finish line. It will look like bold prayers and self-compassion and failed first dates. Moving forward isn't about overcoming your fears; it's about seeking God in the midst of them and having the courage to persevere.

LET YOUR MESS BE YOUR MESSAGE

Another powerful practice to help move forward in our pain is to let our mess become our message. As with everything in grief, this is far easier said than done. But from the very beginning, from the first days following Ben's death, I prayed that God would use my

We can
cherish
what we
had without
comparing
what's to
come.

———

pain for good. In fact, for a long time, it was less of a prayer and more of a demand: *God, you will not let my pain be wasted! I can bear it if you promise to give my pain purpose.*

Though I was making a bold and perhaps entitled request, something in me knew that the only pain I could survive would be the kind that helped others survive their own. It wasn't because I am valiant or selfless or stronger than other people. It was simply the only hopeful template for suffering I could find. In earlier chapters we talked about Joseph's and Ruth's and Job's suffering and how suffering steadied their faiths and glorified God. We see the same thing with the apostle Paul, a previously self-righteous Pharisee who chased down and slaughtered Christ followers in the first century.

After Jesus opened Paul's eyes to the truth of the gospel, Acts tells us this about Paul's call to ministry: "But the Lord said to him, 'Go, for he is a chosen instrument of mine to carry my name before the Gentiles and kings and the children of Israel. For I will show him *how much he must suffer* for the sake of my name'" (9:15–16, emphasis added).

The man who would come to author half of the New Testament and be the pioneering voice of salvation through Jesus Christ to all the Gentile world had to suffer endless messes in order for his message to reach its full potential. The Bible tells us Paul was beaten, stoned, shipwrecked, imprisoned, in danger from every sort of people group, homeless, sleepless, and without food (2 Corinthians 11:25–27) and that he was "so utterly burdened beyond [his] strength that [he] despaired of life itself" (2 Corinthians 1:8).

What Paul experienced is beyond my imagination, and he admitted clear as day he was depressed to the point of wishing for death. And yet in the midst of his persecution and hunger and physical pain, he never allowed his mess to quiet his message. In fact, his suffering made the cry of hope in Jesus even louder for those to whom he witnessed.

We have this chance too, friends. No matter what you're suffering or what you've lost, there are countless others, believers and nonbelievers, who have been or will be exactly where you are. One of the most redemptive and restorative ways we will move forward in our pain is to let our mess become a message of hope to those who can't see hope themselves. I love what Pastor Levi Lusko says in his book *Through the Eyes of a Lion*: "The things God deposits in your spirit in the midst of suffering are the same things that someday other people will desperately need."[3]

Every word between these pages is a deposit from the Holy Spirit given during different stages of my suffering. These words are stained with my tears that I pray will help dry a few of yours. Whatever you're walking through, God deeply desires to deposit his hope and truth in you so that you can do the same for others. Hear me: sharing our stories and sorrow will never be easy. Doing so is vulnerable and brave and will often thrust your heart back into painful places. But testifying is also one of our greatest callings as Christ followers. It is our mission, just as it was for Jesus and Paul and countless others, to let God use our mess to spread the ultimate good message—the one of redemption and hope in Jesus Christ.

Most of our testimonies through suffering won't look like Paul's—thank God! They may not turn into a book or a ministry of any kind. But God will leverage your suffering to be the exact message that the woman down the street or the man in your office desperately needs to hear if you're willing to share your hurt and your hope with them. Your story matters. Your pain is important. And your mess can be used not just to bring light to others who suffer but ultimately to yield purpose and momentum and divine opportunities for your life to continue moving forward.

ten

ADJUSTING MY VISION

WHERE IS OUR HOPE?

But we do not want you to be
uninformed, brothers, about those who
are asleep, that you may not grieve
as others do who have no hope.

1 THESSALONIANS 4:13

N early every question asked, scripture shared, and story told
throughout this book is intended to offer one thing: hope.
Hope for those who've watched a loved one be lowered into the
ground. Hope for those who've lost a marriage because the spouse
chose to leave. Hope for those who feel stuck or helpless or burdened in a home or situation or relationship that seems completely

out of their hands to fix. Hope for all of us who live in a world filled with lemons on Friday.

We've talked about rest and prayer and surrender. We've talked about time's role in our healing and God's role in our suffering. We've admitted how loss of any kind is life-upending and that it often leaves us feeling like we've lost parts of ourselves too. We've talked about how to hold the past and embrace the future, how to move forward. Every one of these ideas is crucial to my daily search for hope in the midst of heartbreak. But if it came down to one assurance I could offer you as you grieve the lemons in your own life? Well, I bet by this point you know my answer.

Jesus—the grace-oozing, strength-giving, soul-redeeming person of Jesus—is the ultimate place from which all hope comes.

He is why we can rest, pray, and surrender. He is the one who suffered so we don't have to suffer alone or in despair. He is the one who is yesterday, today, and tomorrow, who holds the hurts of our pasts and the blessings of our futures in his mighty hands. He is the one we trust when all hope seems lost and goodness feels hard to find. He is the light that shines in the darkness, and he can turn our eyes from all that pains us to all that awaits us if we will let him adjust our vision.

EYES ON THE PRIZE

When Ben and I got engaged, I immediately started painting a rosy picture in my mind of what our life together might be like. Just moments after his "Will you marry me?" and my emphatic "Yes," we both began to revel in the future that we finally knew was certain to come. Sure, we'd talked about getting married, but until he slipped that ring on my finger and we picked out a date and called our families, it was a down-the-road kind of dream.

The ring changed everything. My vision was no longer set on our past or even in our present but was solely consumed and blissfully preoccupied with what was to come. And though I cherished the months of our engagement, the promise of a true, unbreakable, covenant marriage to come was all I could think about. It suddenly seemed that our choices, plans, prayers, and conversations were all centered around the final, anticipated "I do." We even joked with each other over the course of those months, saying, "What on earth will we talk about when this is over?"

Even so, being engrossed in and living for this next phase didn't change the reality of our relationship. Our day-to-day looked similar, our disagreements were very much the same, and the routines we'd established continued to run their habitual course. Planning for our future didn't make everything in our day-to-day relationship easy peasy all of a sudden, but it did cloak the mundane in anticipation of what was coming. What changed with the promise of a secured future wasn't our reality; what changed was our vision.

STRAINING TO SEE THE LIGHT

We've all seen that dualistic, black-and-white image, the one that causes half the observers to see a frowning old lady and the other half to see a young woman with long, Cinderella-like hair. The image itself never changes, but our perception of it does, depending on how long, how carefully, or in what kind of light we look at it. Have you ever found yourself frustrated by this? Angry that what

151

others see as pleasant, youthful beauty you can only see as haggard and without charm?

I'd be willing to bet more of us see the old woman, the grimmer side of whatever season or struggle we find ourselves in. We grow more and more discouraged, straining and striving to see the beauty but staying defeatedly stuck on the hag. For a long time, that's what I saw. I saw an empty bed and an untouched closet full of things that Ben had worn just a few months before. I saw closed law books and dirty boots and a workbench littered with tools that no longer had anything to fix. I saw everything about my life that was empty and everything about my future that had been snatched away. I knew there had to be goodness and beauty even in my season of grieving, but at times I struggled to see it.

Grieving can't be tackled with a glass-half-empty or glass-half-full approach. When life breaks our hearts, our reaction to the pain is far more complex than that. The ugliness of our circumstances is 100 percent real, yet the beauty of God's redemptive promises to us in the midst of those circumstances is just as real. Accepting both of these sides of the picture is the most honest and most helpful way to endure the hardships we face.

The danger comes in focusing too heavily on one side or the other. Allowing myself to be consumed by only the pain gives power to death and control to the Enemy. On the other hand, suppressing or ignoring the pain doesn't serve me either. It robs me of my humanness and stunts real opportunities for healing and growth. I had to learn to see the dark *and* the light—to admit to myself that the present is ugly but my future and the truth of what is to come is infinitely beautiful. In the hands of Jesus, lemons on Friday *will* turn to lemonade on Sunday; we're just not there yet.

It's true that in your struggle, your circumstances might not change. Your sickness might not subside, your child might not forgive you, and your spouse might never come back. But we can adjust our vision. We can keep our eyes on eternity without ignoring the now.

What does this look like in practical terms? For me it looked like two things.

1. I pled with God to give me a vision of Ben at peace with Jesus.
2. I studied heaven.

I asked God daily to let me see Ben with Christ. I wanted just a glimpse of the inexplicable joy he was basking in. Remember all those dreams our friends and family were having? I wanted one too. For the first several months, I got no such gift, but I didn't stop asking, *Lord, please just let me see him.*

In the meantime, I studied heaven. I pored over everything I could find about it, desperate for a true, vibrant picture of what Ben was experiencing so I could start to see the picture of my own life differently. I read an exquisite memoir from the 1800s called *My Dream of Heaven* by a woman who'd chronicled her near-death experience of being in heaven, as well as a similar work called *Imagine Heaven* by John Burke. I steeped myself in Randy Alcorn's five-hundred-plus-page work, *Heaven*, which explains what Scripture suggests about the Christian afterlife. The testimonies and passages these books offered gave my floundering heart a solid place to land. And while the Bible does not give definitive answers about many elements of heaven, I found incredible comfort in one recurring concept.

Though some picture heaven as hyperethereal and disconnected from life on earth, Scripture reveals quite the opposite. We will see familiar people and do familiar things, just as Jesus physically ate and drank with his disciples after his resurrection (John 21:4–14). Also remember Jesus' assurance at his crucifixion to the thief who placed faith in him while hanging on the cross at his side: "Truly, I say to you, today you will be with me in paradise" (Luke 23:43). Will the thief look in paradise as he did in his earthly body? Or will he have a spiritual body, as 1 Corinthians describes: "If there is a natural body, there is also a spiritual body" (15:44)? Whichever it is, we can't know for sure until we're there. But all these passages suggest that we'll know one another in eternity, and we'll likely be aware of the ways we related to one another here on earth.

We see yet another picture of continuity between heaven and earth when Moses and Elijah appeared with Jesus at his trans-figuration. Randy Alcorn explains: "When Moses and Elijah appeared out of Heaven to stand with Christ at his transfiguration [Matthew 17:1–4], the disciples with Christ recognized Moses and Elijah as the distinct individuals they were, the same men they were on Earth, infused with holiness."[1]

It's important to remind you here, I am not a pastor or theo-logian. I am a young widow who is clinging to what Scripture says about heaven because I know my husband is there. I believe these biblical depictions of eternity are true, but I also must remember that all of God's ways are ultimately a mystery to us (Romans 11:33–34; Ephesians 3:4; Colossians 2:2). Ecclesiastes says, "He has put eter-nity into man's heart, yet so that he cannot find out what God has done from the beginning to the end" (3:11). We cannot compre-hend heaven fully through human understanding, but we can find peace in what the Bible does say about it.

Refocusing on the scriptural truths about where Ben is, who he still is, and that my spiritual body (whatever that looks like!) will one day see him again and meet Jesus face-to-face changed the way I looked at my loss. Life without him was still dark, but clinging to the promise of eternity together with Christ brought much-needed light. I had to learn to live with a long-term perspective; to walk with feet on this earth and with eyes on heaven; to acknowledge the dark but remember the light. As I continued to pursue biblical truths about heaven, as I asked and sought and knocked, as the Bible tells us to, the Lord showed up for me in the most incredible way I've ever experienced.

LIVING IN LIGHT OF ETERNITY

It was almost Christmas—the first since Ben's passing. Ben's parents came in town, and we spent time out at the river with my family. It didn't feel like Christmas, but we tried to go through the motions: decorated fireplaces, made sausage balls, exchanged gifts. I've never been one to open presents early or sneak around from closet to closet shaking boxes, but on the night of December 22, a gift came early. And this gift, this divinely delivered assurance from the Lord, was the only gift I needed.

> The dream has a blurry start. I'm in an ambiguous place that part of me recognizes, but it still feels unfamiliar. There are a few girls I know around me, but I feel unsettled. A few of us get in a van and pull up to what I think is an old bar we used to go to. We get out, and there's a nasty storm—sleeting ice, wind blowing benches over, the whole thing.
>
> We walk up this long outdoor corridor with stairs leading

up to what would be the bar. Large wooden beams frame the top of the walkway, and stunning blue gemstones adorn every step, deep like the color of sapphire. I tell the girls I've always loved this place, but then I realize it's actually a place I've never been before. I climb to the top of the stairs, and the girls are gone. The storm has stopped, and it is sunny everywhere, but not in a way that hurts your eyes or demands sunglasses. It is a soft, all-consuming glow.

I walk out onto a grassy hilltop and find myself standing in a strange, open-air shop, kind of like a local market Ben and I shopped at in the Bahamas with my family just six months before. I see Mark, Ben's dad, shopping around, so I go to say hi. He's grinning ear to ear. He looks over my shoulder, staring through me as if not seeing me at all, and gives a huge, excited wave. "Hey, Tonious!" he yells. That's the nickname he always called Ben.

I turn around, and it's Ben! Healthy and normal and smiling, making small talk with everyone in the store. He comes over to me, and I hug him, holding him like I'll never again let go. I ask what he's doing here, and he's evasive, never really giving me an answer. He hugs Mark, too, and shops a little himself. He pulls down a red-and-black plaid flannel shirt. "How about this one?" He turns to me and holds it up.

My knee-jerk reaction is what it always has been: "Ben, you have two just like it." He puts it back, seeming somewhat disappointed. I'm immediately pained with the regret of moments I dismissed him while he was still here. So I make him a deal. "Keep the shirt, but you have to stay with me another week."

In true Ben fashion, he starts to playfully argue about why he can't. I plead a little more, then he pulls from his pocket something that almost looks like a train ticket. It has a date on it: September 18, 2018. He looks up at me, smiles, and says, "You know what? It looks like I've got one more week before the season starts." Opening day of bow season is the following week, and any deer hunter would be eagerly awaiting it, so this doesn't seem out of place for him to comment on.

Ben stays with me, and we leave the shop. Then we're strolling along together in the middle of open, beautiful rolling hills. Nature is everywhere. It looks like the plains of Africa, where we spent part of our honeymoon. It's just us. We aren't even really talking. Sometimes Ben's with me, and sometimes he's somewhere else, but I somehow know he's never gone. I feel him constantly. Even when I can't see him, I know he is holding up his end of the deal, staying with me a little longer as he promised. I have no concept of time, but nothing feels rushed.

After some time exploring, I go up a little hill with a stream flowing down it. There are doves flocking overhead and seven turkeys racing by that are being chased by a big pack of yellow Labs, all significantly smaller than normal size, just like our Ryman is. When I come up over the little hump in the hill, Ben is up there, and for some reason he has no shirt on. Maybe he got hot in the flannel? Another man with dark hair is standing beside him; the man is ambiguous in the face but seemingly quiet and strong. They are clearly best friends. As at least twenty yellow Labs race by, Ben elbows the man, reaches down, and snatches up one pup with a slim little red collar and tells him, beaming with pride, "This one's my girl!"

In a blink the other man, who I now know for certain is Jesus, is gone. The animals are gone, too, and Ben and I stand at the top of the hill. It's peaceful. He says he has to go, and I beg him to stay, that the time he promised me isn't up yet. He gives no explanation, just softly shakes his head no and says he has to go. He says I'll be okay.

As he turns to leave, I see deep, red marks that look like lashes all down his back. They're not raw as if new but are almost like scars that have long been healed. I'm scared and reach out to touch them. "Where did these come from? What happened?"

Ben looks back over his shoulder, then turns to face me once more. He lays his hands over mine and says, "Mattie, it's the coolest story. I know you already know it."

I woke with a jolt, overwhelmed by what I'd just seen, and jumped up. I was anxious to record the dream's details, but processing it seemed impossible without some coffee. So I stumbled around the dark guest room of my parents' river house where we were staying, trying not to wake my sister, who was still sleeping. I grabbed some sweats and a long-sleeved shirt from my overnight bag and snuck out into the hallway. And by the soft dawn glow through the big bay window, I saw the shirt I'd blindly grabbed, the only flannel I'd packed. It was Ben's—the exact red-and-black checkered flannel that he'd bought at the market in the dream. Overwhelmed by this tangible God nod that assured me the dream was from the Lord, I hurried downstairs to grab some coffee and scribble down the details of this unbelievable Christmas story. *Finally!* I thought. *And it was even greater than I imagined.*

While I've never really understood the purpose of the little shop where my tour of heaven began, the sweetness of that scene was simple. It was one last glimpse at the reality of who Ben was—a constant light and friend. Talking and joking with strangers. Hugging his dad with a slap-your-back bear hug, the way he always greeted friends and family. Holding me as if everything were all right, as if I'd never lost him.

As for the cryptic date he pulled from his pocket—September 18, 2018—I realized immediately, as Ben would have, this date fell just before the start of bow season. But what the Holy Spirit revealed to me was that this date referred to much more than just the last week before hunting season. It was assurance from the Father that in the time between Ben's death and his burial (September 12, 2018, to September 17, 2018), I hadn't been alone. Though I know with certainty that when Ben took his last breath on earth, he took his first breath with the Lord (Luke 23:43; 2 Corinthians 5:5–8), in the emptiness of the week from his death to his burial, the Holy Spirit felt closer to me than he's ever been. Maybe during that week, Ben had been watching over me like Moses and Elijah looked down on the disciples. Or maybe the date was yet another specific reminder that Jesus himself was with me, and he will never leave or forsake me.

Perhaps one of the most peaceful scenes from the dream came atop that little hill, where Ben stood fully in his element amid nature, animals, and Jesus. As I replayed the scene in my mind, I almost giggled at the memory of doves flying overhead, biblical emblems of peace and the presence of the Holy Spirit; the seven turkeys running by, as they had in my neighbor's driveway a few weeks earlier; and the darting herd of little Lab puppies just like the one Ben and I had brought home a few months before. Even the one Ben picked up and showed off to Jesus as "his girl" had the same little red collar our Ryman wore.

I found in these details two sweet reminders that have continued to console me since. First, our passions on earth aren't washed away in heaven; they are simply made better. Second, and most importantly, those we love who go before us to paradise can and do still see us and cheer for us and champion us on earth, just as Moses and Elijah did. If Ben could see, pick out, and brag on our sweet puppy from Jesus' side, he sure as heck can see, pray for, and fight for me too. Whoever you love who's gone ahead of you can do that too.

As the dream concluded and Ben turned to leave, I was given the final, physical confirmation that Ben is cloaked fully in every blessing, promise, and redemptive glory of Jesus. I'd seen parts of this picture during his days in the hospital, but the stripes on his back were the last piece of the puzzle. Within Ben's last hours, he started to get worse. The twelve days of being run by machines became too much for his heart to handle, and a blood clot formed, broke off, and stopped all blood flow to his brain. The man I'd been told would be coming back to consciousness in a few hours experienced multiple strokes and was all of a sudden brain-dead. His body was there, but his mind was gone.

There was no way to process that information. No way to make sense of it. All I could think was: *Is he still in pain or is he at peace? Is his spirit still here or has he already gone home?* But as I stared down at my husband, who I knew was teetering between here and eternity, the Lord didn't ask me to process or understand. He asked me to look down—to recognize physical signs on Ben's flesh reminding me that today he would be in paradise. The Bible says when we're redeemed by Christ we literally *become* his righteousness (2 Corinthians 5:21). Not only was that true spiritually for Ben, but I could also see physical marks all over his body reflecting the wounds Jesus suffered during his crucifixion. His hands had holes in them from all the IVs; his feet were marked with Xs from machines that had kept his blood circulating while he was in a coma; a hole from a large chest tube was left in his side just below his ribs; and around his entire head was a crown of thorns—nearly 360 degrees of staples that lined his skull as a result of two brain surgeries.

As graphic as it may sound, and as horrific as it would have looked to most people had they seen Ben like this, there was no more beautiful assurance for me on that day. Not only did I know where my beloved was going, I saw on his physical body exactly what God saw as Ben made his way to eternity. All the Father saw when he looked at Ben was Jesus. And with the final mark of assurance, the stripes on his back that I couldn't have seen with him lying in a hospital bed, I knew now they were there too. I could rest. Every fiber of the man I love was covered with Christ, justified in his image, and now glorified in his presence. He literally had become the righteousness of God.

This dream changed my vision.

I wish I could say Christmas, New Year's, and the rest of that first year without Ben were easier after this dream. They weren't. But I was finally able and willing to see the prettier side of the picture. I could see the light. I was no longer fixated on an image where life is dark and I'm a widow but one where the darkness I can't change is side by side with the light of the Savior who changes everything. Once I was able to see this magnificent end to Ben's story, I began to see a little more hope for my own.

If you, too, are dealing with the death of a loved one—your husband, your wife, your child, your parent—this is their story if they know Christ. This is the fairy-tale ending that is now their reality and will be your reality for eternity too. Steep your soul in that! This truth will adjust your vision and enable you to see some goodness even in the heartbreak. It will sow in you an unexplainable peace in the midst of unconquerable sadness. It will bring you back to life, little by little, and it will slowly redeem what you've lost until you're able to join your beloved again in the grand eternity they've found.

As I've reminded you from page one, this book is *my* story. I simply want to share what's true about my experience and what's true about God. If your story leaves you grieving someone who may not have known Christ, you may have questions concerning eternity that I am not equipped to answer. But I encourage you, take those concerns to a trusted pastor and always, always take them to the Lord in prayer. And as you ask tough questions and prayerfully pursue resolution, don't forget: every bit of the comfort and peace and healing presence of the Holy Spirit is yours for the taking.

You may or may not receive such a clear picture or dream from the Lord, but keep seeking his guidance, his Word, and his presence. Even if you're not sure whether the one you've lost was a believer, keep pursuing the Lord. There is nothing more powerful to bring joy and hope and peace in your suffering than Jesus himself. I know this from experience! I know this because it's true. His promises are true for you if you believe in him, and he is ready and willing to show you. He is ready and willing to meet you in your darkest place, where all you can see is the hag. He is mightily capable of adjusting your vision to see painful earthly realities through the lens of his miraculous eternal one.

I now understand that living in light of eternity doesn't mean reverently, stagnantly waiting for it. No, living in light of eternity means being so desperate for Jesus and so joyful for loved ones who already have unhindered access to him that you can no longer separate this life from that one. Ben isn't gone or lost while I'm left awaiting a far-off day we'll finally converse again above the clouds. He's simply already boarded the plane, and I'm stuck in

The darkness
I can't change
is side by side
with the light
of the Savior
who changes
everything.

————

security. But he and Jesus are saving my seat, ordering me a drink, and demanding the pilot hold on—because someone very special is coming who has a place right beside them.

Living in light of eternity doesn't mean denying realities of life. It doesn't mean I can feel Ben's embrace or hear him speak to me. It means I know that the all-merciful Savior is delighted to continue to share Ben's spirit with me. It means our prayers to have a Christ-centered marriage didn't fully die with Ben. It means the more I surrender what Ben and I had, the more Jesus fills my open hands and broken heart with himself. He is the one I can never lose and the one who's keeping Ben company until it's my time to join them both at home. Hurt and hope, longing and laughing, devastation and anticipation can all happen at the same time in the same heart when Christ is at the center. As much as we may hate today, we have infinitely more reasons to look forward to tomorrow.

THESE WORDS ARE TRUSTWORTHY AND TRUE

I pray that whatever you need from the Lord to start adjusting your vision, you will find it. It may not be a dream, and it may take much longer to receive and look different than you expect, but I believe our God is faithful. I believe in the power of the same Spirit who raised Jesus from the dead to enable us to live into the lighter side of the picture, even when we feel very much in the dark. He is where our hope comes from.

If you've walked the path of tragic loss or you're grasping for some trust in a God who didn't give you the miracle you wanted, cling tight to all that I've walked through and shared in these pages. They were written not for self-help or to mitigate the real despair this life can bring. They were written because they are true of my story and true about who God is. Being honest about my pain and surrendering my grief has revealed volumes about how radically the Lord wants to work in all of our lives, particularly in the seasons of suffering. He won't give us platitudes and pep talks to help us survive our pain but is actively waiting to sustain us, carry us, and help us thrive in the midst of it.

Trusting the Lord in the wake of any loss will be hard. It will be a daily choice as you journey through the valley of the shadow of death. It will come with lots of setbacks and mistakes. You will have to change your perspective and resist the temptation to make God prove that he's trustworthy. He is worth all of your trust. Even in the moments that feel silent and unsure, he is busy at work on your soul and on your future. He is worth handing your suffering over to and resolving to place your trust in. The extent of his hands on your life is impossible to explain but outlandishly awesome when you experience it firsthand.

Jesus may not change your circumstance, nor does he change your heart quickly, but he is the only true way to heal. And you will heal when you pursue him with what Eugene Peterson described as "a long obedience in the same direction."[2] When you choose to trust him and hand over your hurt to him twenty-four hours at a time, one day you will wake up and wonder how you've endured this long, grown this much, and felt the love of Christ in such rich, life-changing ways. You will smile a little bit more than you cry when you think about the one you've lost. And you'll actually be thankful for their sake that they've made it to the home you and I are still waiting for.

Nothing will make less sense to the world than us praising and trusting a God who let us lose and hurt so deeply. But this is our work. This is our testimony. And with it comes great reward. Nothing is more glorious than the radical love with which Christ draws near to the brokenhearted (Psalm 34:18). I would never have chosen this story for my life, and I hate that it may be yours as well. But please take heart knowing that even in your pain, *especially* in your pain, you are perfectly chosen, loved, and cared for by the God of living hope. If you let him, he will tenderly provide everything you need in your struggle and in your healing. He is infinitely greater than what you've lost. And he is here, weeping and waiting for you to adjust your vision, surrender your sorrow, and let him turn your most sour lemons into eternally sweet lemonade.

STAY READY SO YOU AIN'T GOTTA GET READY

The first and only Christmas Ben and I spent together as man and wife was undoubtedly the best of my life—and we had some pretty amazing Christmases at the Jackson house! I remember pestering Ben about what he wanted and researching ideas and racking my brain for months to find the perfect gift for him. Though I knew he'd say that whatever I picked was "phenomenal," I wanted so badly to make it special—a Christmas to remember.

But as I look back, I couldn't tell you for a million dollars what I ended up getting him. I remember how ecstatic he was about what he got me, and I remember all the little trifles I put in his stocking. I'd grown up watching my parents stuff each other's stockings to the brim with candy and knickknacks and little items that no one else would care about, each of which reflected a specific memory from their decades together. In hopes of establishing this same

Christmas tradition, I thought nearly as much about what to put in Ben's stocking as I did his actual gift, and thanks to Amazon, here's where I arrived:

- miniature flashlight with extra batteries
- three hundred zip ties, one hundred each of three different lengths
- new pocketknife
- beef jerky sticks
- bungee cord with hooks
- three-pack of inexpensive bow ties

The bow ties were the outlier, but the rest of his stocking treats were curated under the theme of "stay ready so you ain't gotta get ready." This was one of the many mantras of Ben Selecman's life. I mocked him for both its redneck verbiage and the fact that it was a blatant excuse to keep his truck filled with junk, but this idea has completely altered the way that I walk out my faith.

Though Ben's motivation to stay ready was so he'd be prepared for any outdoor adventure, I've become driven to stay ready as a follower of Christ. He was hoping to be equipped for an impromptu call from a friend to hit the duck blind or go do some outdoor project; similarly, we need to be ready for the grand adventures that God will call us to in our lives. But from what I've experienced, life brings us hardship just as much as it does adventure.

Friends, life in this broken world is hard. It will throw us curveball after curveball. I've never believed it more than I do now: the greatest service we can do ourselves and our community is to stay ready in our faith so we ain't gotta get ready when hardship happens. And like the zip ties and the bungee cord, the ways that we prepare ourselves to rely on the Lord and stay ready usually aren't very glamorous. In fact, sometimes they're downright boring and might feel like an obligation.

A lot of the ways we worship and build our faith on a daily basis can seem tedious and easy to dismiss or overlook when life gets hectic: *Nothing will change if I don't make church today. Nothing will happen if I can't spare five minutes for prayer this morning. Everything will be fine if I just fix this situation my way instead of bringing it first to God.*

But these little things—the everyday, inexpensive tools in our stockings—are how we will stay ready with the Lord so we ain't gotta get ready when our worst nightmares come true. Whatever daily practices make sense for you, in your season of life, in your personal relationship with Jesus, do them diligently.

We will never arrive fully in our faith walks until we go home for eternity. But our daily posture during life on this earth should be to stay ready—for the good and bad, for the adventures and the hardships that will undoubtedly come. Our calling is to live the way Ben did: to the absolute fullest. Sometimes that looks flashy, like pursuing exciting opportunities or experiencing miraculous blessings. But sometimes it looks like faithfully following a God who allows you to hurt.

I'm here to tell you what Ben would tell you, something I found written in the margin of his Bible not long after he went home. Next to James 4:13–14 ("Come now, you who say, 'Today or tomorrow we will go into such and such a town and spend a year there and trade and make a profit'—yet you do not know what tomorrow will bring"), he'd written the following message:

DO NOT TAKE ANY DAY FOR GRANTED!

Value the zip ties, friends. Put in the grinding, glorious work of getting to personally know your Lord and Savior because when you do, you will be ready for whatever life brings you. It won't make things easy. It won't keep you from hurting and struggling and limping to the finish line of this life. But it will absolutely prepare your mind, spirit, and soul so that when anything God has for you comes, good or bad, you will be ready.

ACKNOWLEDGMENTS

To every person who has prayed for me, cried with me, hoped for me, and walked with me through this tragedy: Thank you. You are more than a friend; you are a hand-chosen, perfectly appointed deliverer of the love of God for me in my suffering.

To everyone who has labored in the making of this book, at any stage of its development: Thank you. Your skills and diligence and commitment to my message have turned a nightmare into a long-awaited dream.

To every widow or widower, at whatever age: You are not alone. Your life isn't over. Your future can still be full. Your God is so, so near.

To everyone facing your own Friday full of lemons: The light is coming. The Lord is fighting for you. Don't ever give up hope.

PRAYER PROMPTS

As we've discussed throughout the book, in seasons of extreme stress or suffering, we can often struggle to find the words, the energy, or even the motivation to pray. Even if we know the God of all comfort is readily available to us as his beloved children, we may not always know where to start the conversation. *Should I pray out loud? What do I ask God for? Do I even know what I need? I've prayed so many prayers already, yet I still feel totally defeated. What's the point?*

I have felt all of these feelings. I know what it's like for your mind and body to feel empty and like the last thing you have energy to do is pray. I know what it's like to utter desperate words to God and wonder if they matter. *Will they really make a difference?*

But there's a few things I want to remind you of as you wrestle with the role of prayer in your suffering, and ultimately, in your healing:

1. Prayer is intended to be personal, not perfect or polished.
2. Prayer is an honest conversation with Jesus, not a performance to prove your faithfulness.
3. Prayer is more about getting into the presence of your Savior (*your* Living Hope) than about fixing your circumstances.
4. Any and all prayers are powerful, both those that feel like rambling word vomit and those that you pray directly from God's word.
5. Any and every prayer ultimately reminds you and calls out to God, "I can't do this alone. I need you."

I hope these ideas offer you a bit of relief if you've felt overwhelmed or unable to get back into prayer rhythms during your own tough season. Prayer is a gift of communication and connection with God, and it should never feel burdensome or like an act to earn his favor. I like to think about it like that first phone call you make to your best friend. Whether you've received exciting or devastating news, you immediately know whom to call, which most trusted person to share the report with. What if Jesus became the first person you called? What if your instinct was to run to him first, pour out your heart, and let him sit with you in whatever you're feeling and facing?

Think about how those first calls to a friend sound. They may sound like shock, anger, devastation, or confusion, but they also feel safe. The person on the other end may not be able to change anything about your circumstance, but they're present and secure and trustworthy to hold your pain and your fear. This is often how prayer in crisis or trial feels. Don't overthink it. Make the call to Jesus. Tell him what's happened and what you're feeling honestly. Talk to him like the safe friend he is.

And if you can't imagine where to begin or even what to say beyond, "Jesus, this is what's happened," don't worry. Romans 8:26–27 tells us that "the Spirit helps us in our weakness. For we do not know what to pray for as we ought, but the Spirit himself intercedes for us with groanings too deep for words. And he who searches hearts knows what is the mind of the Spirit, because the Spirit intercedes for the saints according to the will of God." This is incredible news! This is a promise from God himself that when we are fumbling or forgetful or afraid, the Holy Spirit steps in as our translator to the Father. He pleads our cases and shares all that's in our hearts that we don't know how to share.

Ask the Holy Spirit to intercede for you in ways only he can, and then go to Scripture. There is radical freedom and power in praying God's word back to him.

Before we end our time together, I want to help you do just that. Below are several scriptures that were part of my journey back toward meaningful prayer and open communication with the Lord. Lift these holy words up to God when you don't know what or how to pray. Then feel free to take my subsequent words as your own or speak aloud whatever comes to your heart and mind to your safe and mighty friend, Jesus.

Pro tip! Say your name and make the pronouns personal as you pray these passages. Hear aloud the scripture spoken specifically about you. Romans 10:17 assures us by doing so, we are building our faith: "So faith comes from hearing, and hearing through the word of Christ."

2 THESSALONIANS 2:16–17

Now may our Lord Jesus Christ himself, and God our Father, who loved us and gave us eternal comfort and good hope through grace, comfort your hearts and establish them in every good work and word.

Lord Jesus, thank you that because you love me unconditionally and perfectly, I have access to life-changing comfort and hope. Though I don't feel those things right now, I believe you have the power to pour them into my spirit and I call out to you for all of the comfort, hope, peace, joy, strength, and provision I need.

1 PETER 5:6–11

Humble yourselves, therefore, under the mighty hand of God so that at the proper time he may exalt you, casting all your anxieties on him, because he cares for you. Be sober-minded; be watchful. Your adversary the devil prowls around like a roaring lion, seeking someone to devour. Resist him, firm in your faith, knowing that the same kinds of suffering are being experienced by your brotherhood throughout the world. And after you have suffered a little while, the God of all grace, who has called you to his eternal glory in Christ, will himself restore, confirm, strengthen, and establish you. To him be the dominion forever and ever. Amen.

Lord Jesus, thank you that this pain and anxiety and sorrow are no longer mine to carry. When you took on my every sin on the cross, you took every fear and wound and burden on my behalf, too. You are perfectly able to carry the things that I can't. Thank you that you promise me I am not alone in this. You are with me always and you give me brothers and sisters in faith who, too, have hurt like I am hurting. Connect me with them in divine ways only you can. Let us support one another. Thank you that even in hard seasons, you are actively restoring my losses, confirming my righteousness in Christ, strengthening my weak spirit, and establishing more and more eternal glory for me as I depend on you. Keep working in me as you lead me toward healing.

2 CORINTHIANS 4:16-18

So we do not lose heart. Though our outer self is wasting away, our inner self is being renewed day by day. For this light momentary affliction is preparing for us an eternal weight of glory beyond all comparison, as we look not to the things that are seen but to the things that are unseen. For the things that are seen are transient, but the things that are unseen are eternal.

Lord Jesus, this feels anything but light; anything but momentary. Many days it feels impossible not to lose heart. But even as I must face the ugliness of my reality, remind me of the glorious eternity you're preparing me for. Change the perspective of my heart and give me an eternal filter through which to see my broken situation. Even if my outer self and this pain can't be "fixed," Lord, renew my mind and my heart and my spirit and help me to cling to unseen treasures of love, joy, peace, patience, kindness, goodness, faithfulness, gentleness, and self-control that you are sowing in me as I struggle. Give me inexplicable hope in what feels like inescapable sadness. Anything is possible with you, Lord.

ROMANS 8:10-11

But if Christ is in you, although the body is dead because of sin, the Spirit is life because of righteousness. If the Spirit of him who raised Jesus from the dead dwells in you, he who raised Christ Jesus from the dead will also give life to your mortal bodies through his Spirit who dwells in you.

Lord Jesus, remind me day by day, moment by moment, that the same exact Holy Spirit that physically raised your body from the dead lives powerfully and actively inside of me. There is no greater strength or might than that of the Spirit who resurrected you so that you could save me. Remind me that that power is mine because of your holiness and your grace. Thank you that endurance and restoration come from the Holy Spirit's work in me and not what I can do for myself.

EPHESIANS 6:10-18

Finally, be strong in the Lord and in the strength of his might. Put on the whole armor of God, that you may be able to stand against the schemes of the devil. For we do not wrestle against flesh and blood, but against the rulers, against the authorities, against the cosmic powers over this present darkness, against the spiritual forces of evil in the heavenly places. Therefore take up the whole armor of God, that you may be able to withstand in the evil day, and having done all, to stand firm. Stand therefore, having fastened on the belt of truth, and having put on the breastplate of righteousness, and, as shoes for your feet, having put on the readiness given by the gospel of peace. In all circumstances take up the shield of faith, with which you can extinguish all the flaming darts of the evil one; and take the helmet of salvation, and the sword of the Spirit, which is the word of God, praying at all times in the Spirit, with all prayer and supplication.

Lord Jesus, I am so weak. I feel constantly under attack from my pain, my fears, and from an overwhelming feeling of help-lessness. I know this is when the enemy wants to strike. But you have defeated Satan. You have crushed the serpent's head, and he has no power over me because I am covered with your redeeming blood. Protect me from his deceit and his shame. Protect me from isolation in my grief and bitterness toward those who may have contributed to it. You have already defeated my real enemy—keep my eyes clear to see his attacks and shut them down in the powerful, victorious name of Jesus.

LUKE 18:1-8

And he told them a parable to the effect that they ought always to pray and not lose heart. He said, "In a certain city there was a judge who neither feared God nor respected man. And there was a widow in that city who kept coming to him and saying, 'Give me justice against my adversary.' For a while he refused, but afterward he said to himself, 'Though I neither fear God nor respect man, yet because this widow keeps bothering me, I will give her justice, so that she will not beat me down by her continual coming.'" And the Lord said, "Hear what the unrighteous judge says. And will not God give justice to his elect, who cry to him day and night? Will he delay long over them? I tell you, he will give justice to them speedily. Nevertheless, when the Son of Man comes, will he find faith on earth?"

Lord Jesus, you told your disciples to pray like this woman, the persistent widow, so I am. You are a perfectly righteous judge, a good Father, and I will keep bringing my pain and my needs and my desires to you. You may not answer my prayers exactly as I want or in timing that feels speedy to me, but I trust you. I won't stop knocking, asking, and seeking your favor. Hear my bold prayers. Honor my persistence in faith as I continue to lay my needs at your merciful, almighty feet. Help me to never lose heart as you listen and work in my life.

And finally, I pray this for you as you continue to bring your worries, your wounds, and your whole, open heart to the Lord:

"That the God of our Lord Jesus Christ, the Father of glory, may give you the Spirit of wisdom and of revelation in the knowledge of him, having the eyes of your hearts enlightened, that you may know what is the hope to which he has called you, what are the riches of his glorious inheritance in the saints, and what is the immeasurable greatness of his power toward us who believe." (Ephesians 1:17–19)

NOTES

CHAPTER 2: PUMPKINS AND PORCHES

1. Blue Letter Bible Lexicon, s.v. "katapausis (II)," Strong's G2663, https://www.blueletterbible.org/lang/lexicon/lexicon.cfm?t=kjv&strongs=g2663.

CHAPTER 3: FIRST STEPS

1. *Dead Poets Society*, directed by Peter Weir, staring Robin Williams (Burbank, CA: Touchstone Pictures, 1989), 25:45.

CHAPTER 4: GOD NODS AND TREE STANDS

1. Steve and Sarah Berger, *Have Heart: Bridging the Gulf Between Heaven and Earth* (Franklin, TN: Grace Chapel, 2010), 117.
2. Berger, *Have Heart*, 113.

CHAPTER 8: HEAD UP, HANDS OFF

1. C. S. Lewis, *A Grief Observed* (Greenwich, CT: Seabury Press, 1961; New York: HarperOne, 2001), 44–45. Citations refer to the HarperOne edition.
2. Lewis, *A Grief Observed*, 26.
3. Lysa TerKeurst (@OfficialLysa), "Have you ever found yourself saying,

'I don't want this to be my story'?," Facebook photo, September 8, 2019, https://www.facebook.com/OfficialLysa/photos/10156489552547694/.

CHAPTER 9: ROOTS AND WINGS

1. Lysa TerKeurst, *It's Not Supposed to Be This Way* (Nashville, TN: Nelson Books, 2018), 17.
2. *Sweet Home Alabama*, directed by Andy Tennant, starring Reese Witherspoon and Josh Lucas (Burbank, CA: Touchstone Pictures, 2002), 1:06:36, DVD.
3. Levi Lusko, *Through the Eyes of a Lion: Facing Impossible Pain, Finding Incredible Power* (Nashville, TN: W Publishing Group, 2015), 112.

CHAPTER 10: ADJUSTING MY VISION

1. Randy Alcorn, *Heaven* (Carol Stream, IL: Tyndale House Publishers, 2004), 274.
2. Eugene H. Peterson, *A Long Obedience in the Same Direction: Discipleship in an Instant Society* (Downers Grove, IL: InterVarsity Press, 1980).

ABOUT THE AUTHOR

MATTIE JACKSON SELECMAN is a certified sommelier and previously owned a wine bar in Nashville. She also has a degree in creative writing from the University of Tennessee. Tragically, she lost her husband of less than a year, Ben Selecman, in September 2018 after he suffered a traumatic brain injury while on vacation in Florida. Despite her grief, Mattie is pushing forward and has dedicated herself to helping others. Mattie and her business partner, Brooke Tometich, started a philanthropic merchandise brand dubbed "NaSHEville" in order to help women and children in need—specifically orphans, widows, and trafficked women.